THE LIVELY
SHADOW

Also by Donald M. Murray

THE LIVELY SHADOW

Living with the Death of a Child

—⁓—

DONALD M. MURRAY

BALLANTINE BOOKS

NEW YORK

A Ballantine Book
Published by The Ballantine Publishing Group

Copyright © 2003 by Donald M. Murray

www.ballantinebooks.com

Library of Congress Cataloging-in-Publication Data is available from the publisher upon request.

ISBN 0-345-44984-3

Text design by Laura Lindgren

Manufactured in the United States of America

First Edition: February 2003

10   9   8   7   6   5   4   3   2   1

In memory of Lee,
and with appreciation for the efforts of
Dr. James Tucker of Exeter Hospital and
Dr. Daniel Shannon of Massachusetts General Hospital
and all their staffs who fought so hard
to save her

CONTENTS

Survival

Life gives writers the stories they must tell when their long apprenticeship gives them the craft. One of the most elemental stories of mankind, told and retold through millennia in languages we no longer hear, is the story of the loss of a child. Twenty-five years ago life gave me the story of Lee, my daughter, who at age twenty fought Reye's syndrome and lost.

All through the terrible, blurred four and a half days of her dying I kept recording external and internal specific details in my mind as if I would write this story. I was horrified. I was a reporter to my daughter's death. I keep remembering what Guy de Maupassant said about being a writer: "For him no simple feeling exists. All that he sees, his joys, his pleasures, his suffering, his despair, all instantaneously become objects of observation.... He has not a spark of enthusiasm, not a cry, not a kiss that is spontaneous, not one instantaneous action done merely because it must be done, unconsciously, without understanding, without writing it down afterward. He says to himself as he leaves the cemetery where he has left the being he loved most in the world; it is curious what I felt."

Dr. Daniel Shannon opened a family meeting at the hospital six weeks after Lee's death by saying, "You must write this story." My family agreed, but I could not imagine doing it. Yet, from time to time, an uninvited poem would arrive. Then in 1986 I began to write a column for the *Boston Globe* in which I assigned myself to cover the aging process by observing my wife's and my own aging and also recording my own emotional and intellectual response to that aging. There were columns about losing Lee, and they always brought an intense and immediate reader response. After fourteen years of column writing, I wrote *My Twice-Lived Life*, a memoir in which I recounted the lives I have lived and my response to those lives. I passed over the most important experience of my life in six pages. I was not yet ready to respond to Dr. Shannon's command.

Now I must tell my story, but it is only mine. I have not interviewed my wife, my two surviving daughters, Lee's boyfriend, Paul Lambert, or the nurses and doctors who wept when her brain waves ran flat. This is not an objective case history but the individual story of one man who lost a daughter and survived. In telling the stories that must be told, storytellers inform themselves, and when the story is shared, their readers discover their own stories. As they read my story they hear their own, and as we share these stories we survive our lives.

*Lee Murray as a
high school senior in 1975*

1. The Gift

I set the alarm for five-thirty every morning. If I sleep later, I may once more live this dream.

The nurses, doctors, and technicians move away from the bed where Lee, my twenty-year-old daughter, lies in a large room in pediatric intensive care at Massachusetts General Hospital. Lee has been in the care of gleaming stainless-steel machines, left standing where they have last been used. I'm sure my Lee has received the benefits of old-fashioned nursing—a damp cloth to her forehead, the covers smoothed, a gentle touch to her shoulder—but all I see is cold, efficient (but not efficient enough) medical technology, all I hear are the hums, beeps, and blinking lights of electronic monitors.

A large metallic gauge is screwed into her skull. It looks like something that should be attached to a factory furnace. Plastic bags half-filled with potions hang high above her with tubes that loop down like jungle vines to her right forearm. An inappropriate thought comes and passes swiftly like a midnight raid on a village: Lee would find humor in all this machinery—she always found humor in the commonplace—but she will never know all that has happened since she passed into a coma in the ambulance transferring her from Exeter Hospital in New Hampshire to this Boston medical center only four days ago.

I feel as alone as I felt crossing a snow field under hidden enemy eyes in my war years. None of the quiet, lumpily clad medical personnel is there to comfort me. The doctors trained to deliver bad news talked carefully, slowly, patiently, softly to us in the waiting room. Each of us— her sisters, Anne and Hannah; her boyfriend, Paul; her mother—has had moments alone with her. Now it is her father's turn.

I continue to stand at a distance from her bed, where I can see the tubes discreetly hidden under the sheet that carry foul-looking waste into jars below the bed. I follow the wires that lead from her up to the monitors, reading each screen in turn. One shows firm, even, jaunty pulses. That is her heart. One runs a continuous flat line. That is her brain.

I focus on her face, which is as beautiful as ever to me, the face of a middle child who is like and unlike her older sister, like and unlike her younger sister. She is herself, always herself from the beginning, but I see her grandmother and her great-grandmother as if they were shadow photographs, memory pictures, that lay over her face. She is slightly turned away, and yet they led me to this side of her bed. Her cheek at twenty is a woman's cheek, yet still baby soft. Her skin always seemed especially soft, right from the moment I first saw her, washed and cleaned before being presented to her father.

Lee appears untouched by all that has happened to her since she had a fever, took aspirin as she was instructed, fell terribly ill, was diagnosed with Reye's syndrome, and was brought here, where all that could be done has been attempted. Her face is peaceful, ready to wake with a smile. She is as she always will be.

Lee will never grow old, never have wrinkles. Her hair will never gray. She will not grow beautifully into her life, as her mother has, wearing her living on her face. She will not marry Paul or anyone else; she will never have children, never eat another sloppy submarine sandwich, never read again, never laugh, never play her new imported oboe. I will never again hear Albioni being practiced over and over again from the other room. No Mozart, no Bach, no Lee.

I touch her hand, still warm, still alive.

"Lee, I love you. We did all we could.... Goodbye."

I choke on my tears and make myself turn away. I nod the final permission to the staff. I have given her release as I gave my father the gift of death in this same hospital and, two years later in another hospital, gave my mother the death she had so long said she wanted. I see my mother in her corset in my childhood, striding about our flat, beating her fists, chanting "If I had the wings of an angel, over these prison walls I would fly" while I wondered what I had done, what I could do. Well, I finally did it. And now I have done it again, to my daughter who did not want death but life.

I leave the intensive care unit, not even trying to dry my tears, nod to my wife, my daughters, the man who has become a friend but will never be a son-in-law, and then I am asked something. I catch only one word, *autopsy.*

I step back as if I had been slugged, then ask Lee what she would want, hearing her say in my words, "If it would help others."

"It will."

"Then do it," I snapped.

I turn away from the doctor and stand alone, knowing without being told what I must now do. The social worker, a kind, gentle middle-aged woman, leads me down a long corridor, where everyone passing by avoids meeting my eye. She offers me her office, then asks, "Is there anything I can do?"

"Just get the fuck out!" I yell, shocked at how I've suddenly given in to rage, but not apologetic, not then. Her office is at the end of the corridor that leads to intensive care. I call information and get the number of the Deware Brothers Funeral Home, where one brother with a mustache like my uncle Andy's is named Donald Murray Deware. They are Scots Protestant. In times like this we return to our own. The brothers took care of Grandma when I was overseas, then Father, then Mother, now Lee.

I look down the corridor, realizing that as I was dialing

the funeral home, Lee was not dead yet. They hadn't pulled the plug, turned the switch, or done whatever they did to the machines that had been giving my daughter artificial life.

I see her sit up on the bed laughing, hopping down from the bed, racing down the corridor to tell me it was all a joke. She isn't going to die. She's alive.

This is the nightmare I may dream if I sleep late, and so for the twenty-five years since that moment I get up in the dark, nod to Lee, and start yet another day of a life made more terrible, more valued since we let her go.

Innocence

2. Conception

At seventy-eight I watch my five-year-old granddaughter, Michaela, fiercely concentrate on her drawing, remember her mother drawing with the same intensity, then remember a book I found a few years after Mother's death that was awarded to her for her drawing in school in Scotland, and wonder if this visual concentration they all share came from Scots fishermen who had to read the sea and sky a thousand years ago, maybe ten thousand. Grandsons Josh and Sam stage a mock fight with sticks picked up in the yard—lunge and parry, slash and counterslash—and I wonder how much this instinct has been passed down through me from the great-great-uncle for whom I was named who took a ball in the leg at Waterloo when he fought against Napoleon with the Black Watch. The last time I saw Grandma Smith, days before I went overseas in World War II, she thought I was that uncle from her childhood and that I was off to fight Napoleon, not Hitler.

Lee, conceived during the ridiculous and sublime act of love on a summer afternoon, was designed by genetic codes formed long ago by ancestors we cannot name because our lineage so quickly disappears into the unrecorded history before history. Back through her mother, Lee was descended from the Germanic tribes who survived on the vast plains that stretched across northern Europe. Some may have been tailors, Jews who came here to escape the army and the old cruel prejudices. Certainly when I see Minnie Mae on her knees planting a garden in the way I saw farmers plant in Germany, I know that many who came before her worked the land. Through me, Lee was the child of farmers and probably fishermen, all Scots, Highland and Lowland, later factory workers and preachers, even a poet and a translator of the New Testament into shorthand for working girls and Hindi for heathens. They all came here after the Great Awakening, Baptists suffering oppression from the Presbyterian Church of Scotland.

I feel the need to trace back these genetic rivers that combined to make Lee the woman she was. I am still a bit surprised that I became a father, a role that has been so central to my life that I cannot imagine it without children. I had never expected to be a parent. My mother should never have been a mother. She had no talent for it and took no pleasure in it. My father was bewildered by his role all his long life. I wasn't against having children; it just never appeared in my plans. I was forever making plans of escape during my childhood, dreaming of faraway lives I might lead. Parenthood was, as I think it is for many men, simply not in the cards.

But then when I first held our firstborn, Anne, in my arms, I knew I was a father. In a matter of seconds, I was fully trained to love and care for this infant daughter. It had not been an easy birth. Minnie Mae had toxemia (also called eclampsia), and the doctors had to induce the birth. At Beth Israel Hospital in Boston I was told that there was a fifty-fifty chance that mother or child would not survive the birth, and if the baby did survive, she would almost certainly be blind.

"Would you like the name of a doctor who could tell you how to tell your wife your daughter is blind–if she and the baby survive?"

"Yes, I guess."

"Dr. Green. He's an expert in the field."

I saw Dr. Green and, of course, discovered there is no good way to tell your wife the baby is blind. Armed only with instinct, I waited in the hospital lobby, seven floors away from my wife, as she went through thirty hours of labor. She was fine, Anne was not blind, but as Dr. Louis Zetzel told me the good news he rapped the back of his hand on my fly and said, "Keep it zipped up."

And zipped up we kept it, although we wanted more children. Then I became a writer at *Time* magazine and Minnie Mae went to a new gynecologist, Dr. Gussberg. He referred Minnie Mae to Dr. Tillman, who had studied Irish Catholic and Orthodox Jewish women who had disobeyed doctor's orders not to have children after suffering toxemia. There was rarely a reoccurrence of toxemia. The idea of the child who became Lee was born.

But conception, so easy with Anne, did not take place. We turned to Dr. Marty Gold, who was truly a family physician. He also treated Minnie Mae's mother, who had moved in with us. His medical advice was, "Go away for a week without mother." We signed up for a farm vacation in Hudson, New Hampshire, and we are certain that Lee was conceived that first afternoon.

Nine months later she arrived in a rush. As the doctor was telling me on the telephone in Minnie Mae's room how long I could expect to wait, I heard the nurses shouting to him that she was already arriving. Our first daughter had had colic and parents who did not know how to calm, feed, or care for a baby, but when Lee arrived we were experienced parents who could read each cry, who knew how to burp and change and nurse a baby. From the beginning she was a sunny child, greeting us in the morning with a smile, laughing at Anne's foolishness and ours. Two years later Hannah arrived, and Lee became the middle child.

After she was gone at twenty we realized how she was central to the family in many ways, close to Anne, three years older, and just as close to Hannah, two years younger. Anne and Hannah were five years apart—Anne's fifteen to Hannah's ten; Anne's high school to Hannah's fifth grade—and were sisters but lived lives far apart from each other. As a middle child, Lee knew how to fit in and, in a way I did not realize until it was too late, disappear into the family, causing few problems and little concern.

As I write this I feel guilty that I didn't know her better, that we didn't design a life that allowed Minnie Mae and me to be alone with each daughter in childhood as much as we are in adulthood. Minnie Mae and I have a close marriage and we had a close family, but although each of us had a distinct personality, I think in our daughters' early years we were a unit, with the middle child most hidden, best able to fit in, and therefore less known.

And yet she was always there, sensitive and resilient, caring and self-directed, the child you knew who would always be there for her sisters and for you in the many years ahead.

3. Our Memories

I don't have a memory book in my mind like a photo album, arranged chronologically and able to be perused season by season: snapshots of Lee at the beach, playing in a pile of leaves, building a snow fort, bringing home a bunch of spring flowers. Her life was woven into the lives of each of us—mother, older sister, younger sister, father—and the images jump about in time. She is a baby, a young woman, a teenager, a girl alive in reality and in memory, each moment a fragment caught out of time passing and held steady. Are the memories accurate? Each is true to me although they have, as all memories, been worn smooth with telling. In twenty-five years they have been changed by frequent handling, as I have feared that Lee would disappear into the past and beyond.

I see Lee sitting on the training pot. My arms are still heavy with carrying her from the car to her bedroom, sound asleep after a long trip. Lee is in her playpen laughing at Anne, her older sister, who is making faces from the freedom of an entire room; Lee is standing outside the playpen making faces at Hannah, her younger sister, who is standing wobbly-legged in the playpen, laughing at Lee.

When we found out who Lee's teacher would be in third grade, her older sister groaned, and we joined in. The teacher was an older woman who was supposed to be tough. Although we didn't approve of parents who did this, Minnie Mae and I volunteered to try to get Lee transferred, but Lee stopped us: "I'd like to give her a chance." It was typical Lee, and she had a good year. The "terrible" teacher became one of her favorites.

When Lee was in high school, Minnie Mae heard that the police had given Lee a hard time about a six-pack of beer. Minnie Mae stomped up to the police station saying that her daughter hadn't had beer, certainly hadn't driven with beer in the car. Later Minnie Mae crept back to the police station and apologized. Lee had been driving our big yellow Chevy Suburban in a parade of victory after a high school soccer or basketball game. Someone had had a six-pack, and Lee had gotten rid of it—by tossing it on the hood of a police car.

Lee called during one of her first weeks at the University of Massachusetts. She had eaten alone in the dining hall, she told us: "I was down and felt sorry for myself. Then I looked around and told myself that all these people had had the chance to eat with an interesting oboe player and they passed it up. Then I was all right."

She was puzzled that people in her women's dorm kept talking about all the JAPs, because she didn't see any Japanese girls. We explained the term "Jewish American princess." We called to share the news we'd bought a new car, and she was delighted. Later she told us that one of the women on her dorm floor had called home and found that the phone was disconnected—her parents had moved and not told her where they were. This really upset Lee, and us.

In her sophomore year, Lee moved into a coed dorm, and soon the Paul we'd been hearing about came to visit.

He blended right into the family in a way that made us understand what it would be like to have sons-in-law. We had known some of Anne's boyfriends, but they kept themselves at a distance or she kept them at a distance. Paul was a biochem student who is now a professor at the University of Wisconsin, where he took his doctorate, and is happily married to a fellow scientist.

When I was discouraged by what I thought were poor student evaluations of my teaching, Lee demanded that I bring them home. She examined them and pointed out how few students didn't like my teaching and how many did. I remember my pain when I tried to comfort Lee about her mid-600s SAT scores by saying they were average. She was outraged: "I am not average."

Some nights I wake and see the back of Lee's head and shoulders where she sat at the end of the bed watching the Olympics on television until late into the night. I look into my woods and she is there with the Stammatels next door or the Aldens before them, and the Driscolls from across the street, trudging down to the edge of Oyster River for another adventure. I am in my office upstairs when we first move in, and the door to the garage is flung open and a line of girls passes through. Lee looks over and gives me a grin.

She is moving away and then returning, laughing in the infant swing we have hung over the door to the kitchen in New Jersey. She is amazed when she is six and we drive through Lee, New Hampshire, on our way to a new home in Durham, the next town over. The German border guard points to her passport, nudges his partner, and pays special attention to Lee, whose middle name is Emmerich for her mother, and we are in the town of Emmerich, and I remember our division headquarters in the rubble in this same place years before Lee was even in my dreams.

I watch Lee and her sisters setting out the tiny cups and plates for a party on the flat stone in the rock wall behind our house, and taste again the rich flavor of a tiny imaginary cup of tea. I stand in the Durham cemetery, where members of the Durham service department moved that same stone so it could become the gravestone when so unexpectedly we needed to buy a cemetery lot for Lee.

I worry about Lee because her face is an unhealthy

red from the heat, 105 degrees, as we hike the bridge back from Tijuana, Mexico, on our trip around the country on my first sabbatical. I remember how shocked she and Hannah were at the children begging. My mind jumps to our walk along a street in New Orleans days before and our uncomfortable and ineffective explanations of what the women were selling as they passed by, more naked in their clothes than they would have been nude. My memory jumps ahead, and Lee is home from a musical trip to Romania and I remember her shock as she tells us how the oboe players she met had been chosen in the Communist system to play the oboe when they were in elementary school. No choice; it was a command. Lee was concerned about her friends, how their parents treated them, what courses they were advised to take or not take that might close doors in the future.

When Lee was a senior in high school she took college-level English with the poet Mekeel McBride and later a humanities course in poetry I team-taught with a poet. There was a special delight in sharing our craft and a secret. Only the other teacher knew of our relationship. Sometimes Lee would show me her work late at night, when I was already in bed, and our joke was that someday she would slip up and say in class, "Last night when I showed you this in bed . . ."

And, of course, Lee visits in dreams. In most dreams I see her alive as a child, a teenager, a young woman, as the mature woman she will never be, yet know at the same time that she is dead and that I am dreaming her alive.

When I had my heart attack and they were losing me, I looked up the long, brightly lit tunnel and there was Lee, in the blue jumper she made, waving.

The kaleidoscope of memories never ends.

4. Lee's Memories

Filled with my memories of Lee, I turn to the shockingly small, messy heap of photos and papers Lee has left behind. I have never, in the twenty-five years since she died, looked at these now faded, often blurred papers. Now it is time. Yet it has been weeks since Minnie Mae handed me the box of Lee's papers. I have avoided it every day I have come to the office. I have moved it so it gets in my way as I head to the desk, but I have not lifted them out of the box and stacked them on my desk. I take a ruler. Only six and half inches of papers for twenty years of life. The urn that holds her ashes in the cemetery was taller.

But behind the avoidance and the bowel-cramping grief, still so fresh, still so hard to confront, is a curiosity. We never opened our daughters' mail, listened in on their phone calls, searched their rooms, read their notebooks or diaries, interrogated them about the lives they lived more and more away from home. Now I am going to invade her privacy, and I have a slight fear of what I may find and a greater question: Will I find the Lee I remember or another person entirely?

I led a secret life in my parents' home. They did not know me, and I hoped the home I made for my own children would not be as filled with the silences, distance, turning away, and subversive privacy of my younger years.

As I open the folders and envelopes that come to my hands, looking at the snapshots and reading the papers, I am struck by their ordinariness. And what wonder there is in the commonplace life.

A color picture of Lee and Paul, heads pushed together to fit the viewfinder, laughing. I can hear the tumbling sounds of their laughter now. A list of activities written roughly, perhaps for her application for college, perhaps for her high school yearbook:

Music: school band, orch. And chorus 1971–73. N.H. All
State 1972 Orch. 1973 band. 1974 orch. All New England
1974 orch. Pit coach for the shows "Oliver" and "Okla-
homa." I played in a UNH quintet for two years. Outing
Club member 1973–75, Drama Club member 1971–75. Sec.
of class 1973–1974, sec. of Latin Club 1973–1974, girls' JV
Basketball Team 1971–1972.

I didn't know—or didn't remember—that Lee was class
secretary.

I run my fingers over handwritten manuscript pages
of her notes for short stories as if I could touch her by
feeling her handwriting. There is a University of New
Hampshire Dairy Bar sales slip from the summers she
worked there. A copy of her paper "The First Bees in
Massachusetts" with a note from Professor Henry Hage-
dorn saying, "I have sent it off to ABJ. Your grade for the
paper was A." We laughed at her taking a beekeeping
class to satisfy a science requirement, but it led to her
first—and only—publication.

I find her letter of admission from the New England
Conservatory of Music with carbons of her letter of acceptance and another carbon turning down her acceptance at

Hartt College of Music. A letter to us on Snoopy stationery about her first day away at college, so wonderfully ordinary it made me cry, so full of the beginning of a long life.

A paper written when she was twelve, perhaps for school, perhaps for herself, that makes me remember what I had forgotten—a soda bottle exploded in the kitchen late one night and created a glorious mess.

> *While cleaning up the mess my mother had to take off a panel on the bottom of the ice box to clean well. The problem, though is trying to get the panel back on. My mother, having tried without success asked my father to do it. My father having a hard time got mad and started hitting the ice box. The ice box, my mother said should not be hit, but my father said it was his and he could do what he liked with it.*
>
> *My mother started laughing, when she realized how funny it was, but couldn't stop. When my father came upstairs he also realized it was funny and started laughing and couldn't stop either. So it all turned out fine.*

Sophomore college grades, notes for a German class, the home address of her roommate, her handwritten memories of the day she sneaked out of the house and stood in the street experiencing rain. A description of her feelings when a conductor ridiculed her and said she made a sound like Niagara Falls on her oboe. A clipped stack of papers she never saw, the Massachusetts General Hospital bill—admission 8/2/77, discharge 8/5/77—and page after page of charges, twenty-one pages in all, for treatments that did not work. A short story she wrote in her fiction-writing class at the University of Massachusetts. A letter to her friend Marty that was never sent. The small black spiral notebook that had belonged to my father and had been saved from my mother's compulsion before his funeral to get rid of everything that had been his. I didn't know she took that notebook on a college trip to perform music in Romania. The Cold War was still hot, and I remember her shock at seeing the pipes sticking up in fields that indicated underground prisons. I also remember her shock at the treatment of Gypsies.

The gypsy is a class below everyone else. They sweep the streets, wash windows, etc. They wear scarfs on their heads, are very poor. Long noses and dark skin.

Years after Lee's death, Mekeel McBride handed me a folder with her high school English papers. I read the first one then, could read no more, and put it away in my files. Now I take them out and make myself read them all. Her normal life becomes extraordinary in the context of her early departure. I hear Lee's voice, her own vision of the world, her sensitivity and evolving toughness. I will allow her, after so many years, to speak.

WHAT I REMEMBER

The first thing I remember is being in a car and looking at a calf standing in a grass triangle in the middle of two country roads.

I don't remember when my little sister appeared because in all my memories she's there. Once I asked my mother if I could change my sister's diapers. My mother peeled off her diapers and said I probably wouldn't like to do it very much.

When I was three years old my parents took my two sisters and me to a huge studio to have our picture taken. The photographer put me on one side of a bench, my older sister who was six on the other side of the bench and my little sister who was one in the middle. My older sister and me smiled but my little sister kept moving around and kicking off her shoes. Finally the photographer took our picture with my little sister frowning and playing with her toes.

One time I did something bad and I knew my mother was going to spank us. So I took the rubber spatula and hid behind a chair in the living room. I took a bite out of the spatula and then I got bored so I gave myself up.

My sisters and me used to play a game where we'd put a blanket in a small suitcase and go downstairs like we were going on a trip. In the downstairs hall we'd spread the blanket out and go to sleep on it as if we were in a hotel. After about a minute one of us would call like a rooster and we'd go upstairs again so we could start the whole game over.

One afternoon my older sister and me decided to get drunk on water. So we got out our dolls' china drank as much water as we could. Instead of feeling good we both felt sick and each time we moved our stomachs would slosh.

My grandmother usually made our breakfast. One time she poured buttermilk on our cereal. It tasted sour and we wouldn't eat it. My mother tried to explain to my grandmother what she had done but I don't think she ever understood.

When I was in kindergarten my mother would meet me out side of the school and walk home with me or she would pick me up in the car so that I wouldn't have to cross the busy streets by myself. We lived in New Jersey when I had stayed late my mother wasn't there to meet me. It scared me but I thought that I should at least start walking so I could meet her on the way. I was sure that she'd come for me. But I still hadn't seen her by the time I got to the last busy street before my house. I didn't want to cross this street by myself because there were so many cars and my mother had told me not to. So I sat on a little rock that was in the corner of a yard and waited for somebody to come and get me. It seemed like hours before I saw my father drive up in the car. As soon as I got into the car I started crying because I had thought everybody had forgotten me.

When I was six we packed all our clothes, furniture and toys into a large truck. The next morning we moved to Durham N.H. My father told us that we probably wouldn't be able to see much T.V. because we were going so far north. It was hot when we got into our green and white rented house. We drank cases of Orange Crush.

I shared a room with my little sister. Instead of picking up anything we just made big piles of clothes and toys in the middle of our room. If my parents told us to clean it up we stuffed the piles under our beds and into the closet.

In my first grade class everybody knew the alphabet except for me. So my mother tried to teach it to me. In the morning when I left for school she'd tell me a letter and ask me to remember it so I could repeat it to her when I came home for lunch. One morning she gave me the letter M. I kept repeating the letter N in my mind as I walked to school. When I got home I proudly said the letter N.

The teacher told us one day in first grade that President Kennedy had been shot. One boy clapped because his parents didn't like Kennedy. The teacher told him to shut up.

My second grade teacher made me stay after school because I rang the bell on her desk. She brought me home and told me what an awful person I was. When she talked to my parents she called me a nice little girl.

I learned to sing Silent Night in Japanese in fourth grade. My fifth grade science teacher was named Mrs. Herrick. We called her Mrs. Hatrack. She made us watch a bat being born.

In the sixth grade I got to go to dances that started at 8 o'clock and ended at 10 o'clock.

My seventh grade history teacher wore low cut dresses. When ever she bent over you could see all the way down her dress. The boys liked her a lot.

In eighth grade everybody wore necklaces with peace symbols on them. We had a strike like they did in college. All the students went outside and yelled strike. The teachers told us if we didn't come back in side that we'd all flunk out. So we went back into the school.

I tried out on my oboe for the N.H. All State Festival when I was a sophomore and got the first seat in the band.

The summer I was sixteen I went to England with my family. In a museum a sixty year old man with bad teeth tried to pick me up. I walked away and five minutes later he was talking to another girl.

When I was a Senior I remembered that when I was in sixth grade I thought seniors were very grown up and mature. I didn't feel that way.

Today I wrote an autobiography for English 401.

I find Lee's autobiography deceptively simple. It is crafted so that the reader sees the world through her eyes at each age. Gradually her world expands; she begins to lose her innocence and becomes reflective.

We lived in the ideal college town, but, as the following paragraphs document, it is not easy to grow up, even in an ideal community. I grow angry at these cruelties I never knew about and want somehow to protect her retroactively, but we cannot protect our children. All we can do is give them the love that will allow them to go forth in the world and have a place of retreat and comfort when necessary.

EMBARRASSING MOMENTS

One day when I was in the second grade the most popular girl in my class came up to me and asked me to her party that Friday night. I was happy that I had been asked and I accepted her offer quickly. Then she told me it was a dress up party. Just as she said dress up she pulled my dress up. The class saw it happen and they started laughing. So I ran into the bathroom and cried.

I was a freshman in high school sitting with a group of friends when a boy who was a junior came over and sat down with us. He was tall, blond and he didn't have a girlfriend. He talked to us about school for a while then he asked if anybody had seen the joke with the nickel. I hadn't so he gave me a nickel and told me to put it on a piece of paper and draw around it with a pencil. I looked up and saw that he was smiling at me. I thought that he might like me. Then he told me to put the nickel sideways on my forehead and to roll it down to the end of my nose. All friends were laughing and I didn't know why until some of the lead on the nickel came off on my fingers and I figured the lead was on my face too. I laughed and hurried to the bathroom when the bell rang. Behind me I heard the boy say, "I didn't think that she'd do it. What a jerk."

When I was a freshman in high school there was this boy I had liked all year. One day in biology he started talking to me about himself and he got me some paper. When the bell rang he followed me out of the classroom and up the stairs. I was so excited that he was walking with me up the stairs that I slipped on the next to top step and all my books fell down the stairs.

The day before I had read a book which said that I would be mature when I learned how to laugh when I'm *embarrassed. So I sat on the stairs for five minutes and laughed hysterically. But instead of the boy telling me how mature I was he told me I was an idiot and walked away.*

Lee was seventeen when she wrote these papers, and the following account is especially poignant, since she would go on to be a music major at the University of Massachusetts and then, when she was twenty, make the decision to lead a life of music. She auditioned for the New England Conservatory of Music and was accepted. I remember her joy at her admission into a school that would test her talent and musicianship and would lead to a career in music—certainly as a musician and perhaps as a composer. In this piece I hear the self-reflective, sensitive voice of the independent, self-disciplined woman Lee was becoming.

THE AUDITION

On the second day of school in my freshman year of high school I walked into the music teacher's office and asked him about trying out for the New Hampshire All State festival. There's a band, orchestra and chorus. Students audi-

tion for a place in one of the groups. If they make it they go in April to some place in N.H. and practice in the group for three days. On the last day they give a concert. The students that make it have to play well.

The music teacher filled out an application and gave me my try out piece. It was the Mozart concerto in C major. It's a very difficult piece. Some of the best oboists in the world have played it. The only way I could possibly play it was if I practiced every day of the six weeks before the audition.

I started out only playing a couple of lines. I kept adding lines to those. Some days I spent half an hour on one run and I still couldn't get it right. I played the piece so many times I could play it from memory. The record I played so much that when I played the oboe part I could hear the orchestra's part in my head. The last week before the audition I went over the piece to polish it up. Now all I could think of was that audition.

The day for the audition came. I put on my best dress because I thought that appearance would count for something.

Since the auditions were in Portsmouth one of the parents of another kid trying out drove the rest of us who were trying out. We were all quiet on the way over. Occasionally one of us would say that they wished they had a couple more weeks which didn't help me relax at all.

We came to the Portsmouth High School, got out of the car and went through the front doors. There was a table with a big sign on it that had REGISTRATION on it. We gave the people at the table our names and they told us which rooms to go to.

We were put into different rooms where there were kids from different schools. I went to my room and picked a desk without a coat on it and sat down. In this room there were about fifteen kids all playing their instruments and showing off. One trumpet player was playing the theme from a T.V. show that had gone off the air two years earlier. There were saxophone players, flute players, bassoon players, clarinet players and one other oboe player.

The girl who played the oboe was short, had long brown hair and wore lots of makeup. She saw me at the same time I saw her. She quickly played her piece of music. I listened but I didn't look like was listening. I'm sure she knew I was listening. So I carefully took my oboe out of the case and put it together. Then I played my piece of music. I looked at her and saw that her head was turned half away from me. I knew that she had heard me. So I convinced myself that I had played better.

When I realized she wasn't going to play again I started fooling around with my reed because I was nervous. The reed of an oboe is very delicate. One day it can be perfect and the next day it won't even play. Also if it soaked too much it will play badly and if it soaked too little it will play badly. I soaked it in some water then I played on it. It still needed to soak a while so I let it sit. After a while I warmed up the reed and the oboe. I kept on soaking the reed because I was bored and before I knew it the reed was too wet. So I put it in the case and told myself not to touch it again before the audition.

My audition was scheduled for 4:10. At 4:05 a man came to the room and called my name. The room quieted down and everybody watched me as I gathered my stuff and followed the man out the door. The man walked quickly down the hall, up some stairs and down another hall. I had to run to keep up with him. He told me to wait until the girl came out and then he disappeared down the hallway.

I was all alone in the dark hall. I could hear the faint

sound of music and voices from the room in front of me. The window in the door of the room had been covered with paper so I couldn't see into the room. I paced the hall, and squeaked on my reed and told myself to do a good job. At last the girl came out and told me the judge was nice and to go in.

The woman didn't even look at me when I walked in. She was writing so I tried not to disturb her. A few minutes later she looked up and told me to play a G major scale. I played it slowly but smoothly because I had practiced it. Then she told me to play a chromatic scale only she told me to start on low F instead of the low C which I always start on. I made about five mistakes on the scale. When I finished I looked at her and saw that she looked bored and I started to shake.

Next she told me to play my solo when I was ready. I took a deep breath and started to play. I was surprised that once I started playing I wasn't nervous anymore and I forgot about the judge. Right before the hardest run she stopped me and I was glad because I couldn't play it. I thought that she would say something but she just smiled and told me to send the next person in.

I walked down the empty hall thinking about what I

could have done better and then I remembered that I had
to wait six weeks before I could find out how I did.

As her autobiography documents, she was made first
oboe in the All State band, another step in a short life in
which she had the support of her parents as she followed
her own goals and achieved them.

Reality

5. The Phone Call

On a hot August afternoon in Vermont in 1977 I pull over to the side of the road to enjoy a landscape in which heat and color rise in van Gogh sunlight. It has been a good summer of teaching and writing, and Minnie Mae and I can now take the time to celebrate the goodness of our life. The sun is so bright it jumps off the rows of yellow-tasseled corn and the green leaves of other crops, rises from the gently rippling meadows, glints from the white houses and passing pickups. The glare from Lake Champlain below the sloping farmland forces me to squint to make out the heeling sailboat far out on the water. Even the dark woods edging the fields, which usually appear dark and forbidding since I fought my war so many years before, seem welcoming, promising cool shade and the pungent odor of pine needles.

We are returning from an afternoon visiting the Shelburne Museum with good friends Betty and Don Graves, the other three of us impressed and amused at Betty's insatiable lust for information. Don, a close friend and colleague at the University of New Hampshire, came to Vermont to give a guest lecture. We both have earned the vacation day. I haven't written as much as I wished— I never do—but the intense teaching at a University of Vermont summer program for teachers of writing went well.

In early spring Paul Escholz had called me to teach in the program and I said no, this was to be a summer of writing. When I hung up, the phone rang again and I heard Lee's ecstatic voice telling me that she had been accepted by the New England Conservatory in oboe and would study with a member of the Boston Symphony Orchestra. The tryout had been tough, but the evaluators had complimented her on her musicianship and welcomed her to join their company.

Lee had always been thoughtful of us. She did not want to waste our money on an expensive conservatory education and a first-class French oboe until she was sure she was ready to dedicate herself to a career in music. So she had completed two years of college, and only this year had she come to a decision to study in one of the best conservatories in the country. She had made this choice with the quiet sureness that was typical of her. Her course was set. She would study oboe, perhaps attempt the cello, possibly try to compose. She would try to play in a major orchestra, but if that didn't work out she would teach and play in local orchestras and chamber groups. We didn't know what she and Paul had decided, but they were remarkably comfortable with each other, spent time with us like old friends, easy in conversation and comfortable with silence. Marriage was not mentioned, but we felt our family was increasing, and we saw their future as they did—Paul would live a life of science and Lee a life of music.

The tuition at the conservatory was going to be much more than we were paying at the University of Massachusetts under an exchange program with the University of New Hampshire, but we reassured Lee that we could afford it. The offer from the University of Vermont for the summer program was to the dollar what the new tuition would be. When I hung up after talking with Lee, I dialed Paul. The offer was still open, and I took it. Things were working out better than we could have imagined.

Now the summer program is just about over, and I am especially proud I earned the money for her education. When I was in high school my father had cashed in the college insurance policy he had bragged about during my childhood. I was not surprised; it was part of a pattern. I saved my own money and was offered a junior college scholarship that covered half the $1,200-a-year cost for tuition, books, and room and board. When I went to the savings bank to withdraw my money, it was gone. Since I was under eighteen years of age, Mother had had access to my account, and she had withdrawn the money. No surprise, no anger. I told the representative from the school what happened, and she arranged both a job and a football scholarship.

I vowed to myself that I would not live my parents' life of debt. I had been forced to participate in its apologies, explanations, made-up stories, and false promises, and felt its humiliation and shame. When my children were ready for college, I would pay their way. Now our oldest daughter, Anne, has graduated from college without debt. Lee has finished two years of college, and the funds for her third year are in the bank. Hannah will soon graduate from high school, and we'll be able to pay her way as well. I am proud, perhaps even a bit smug. I am not my parents. I pay my bills. Lee will be able to follow her dream.

We have another reason to appreciate this moment. Minnie Mae had an enormous natural talent as a mezzo-soprano and was a soloist in Washington, D.C., and Boston, but although her parents sent her brother to college, no one suggested she study at a conservatory or even go to college. Now Lee has the support her mother did not have; Lee will be able to do what her mother was not able to do.

I myself feel a sense of accomplishment. I am not the great poet and fine novelist of my dreams, but I have published articles, poetry, novels, and a textbook on teaching writing, a satisfying act of revenge against my high school English teachers. Despite the fact I have no doctorate, I am chair of the English Department and have been invited to teach at other universities. I am blessed with good friends such at Betty and Don Graves,

48 DONALD M. MURRAY

am still in love with my wife, and have three daughters who are becoming women of a fascinating individuality.

After a lifetime of struggling for achievement, I am trying to learn to take satisfaction in what I have accomplished, but I'm still uncomfortable with pride. My Scots Baptist born-in-sin background doesn't condone pride. As we drive I laugh with Don at our difficulty enjoying this lazy day of relaxation after weeks of work. We are both men of schedules, lists, deadlines, and Yankee Protestant guilt. His mother used to ask, "It's ten o'clock in the morning. What have you done today?" I did become impatient at Betty's museum meandering but told myself I should relax, stroll instead of stride, visit yet another exhibit in the museum's thirty-seven buildings.

We make plans for dinner as we drive back to Burlington, and then as the four of us walk into the house Minnie Mae and I have rented the phone rings. It's Anne. Lee is sick, terribly sick. They don't know what it is, but she's been taken to Exeter Hospital by ambulance.

Minnie Mae and I pack quickly, but it feels slow, oh so slow. Betty and Don help us and promise to bring the rest of our stuff back to Durham.

We apologize. We're overreacting. She has a fever, a

virus or something, and the hospital is the best place for her. They'll know what to do. The girls were right to send her there. We are rushing, hurrying to reach our daughter who is sick, but in our innocence we fear it is serious but do not really believe it can be. We are being overdramatic. Everything will be just fine.

At the same time the dread is real. I feel as if I'm walking in a lake of molasses. We are away from our children, and something terrible has happened. We don't have a name for it. The doctors don't know what's wrong, but she has a fever, she's vomiting, she's so sick they had to call for an ambulance to take her to the hospital.

I reassure Minnie Mae during the drive—again and once again and then again—to reassure myself. This will just be another crisis we will survive—an appendectomy, an infection that just needs a new pill. It will all become a family story: how we were away in Vermont earning the money for Lee's tuition when she got sick and how silly we were rushing back madly to find her back home, laughing at our unnecessary concern, how Mother always was a worrywart, how Father always imagined the worst.

We drive down Route 89, which we have always

thought one of the most beautiful highways in America, but today the lush August landscape is black and gray in my eyes. Distractedly, I pull off 89 at White River Junction to buy gas and coffee. The car is so filled with silence, I think it will explode.

We *are* worriers, and our anxieties come from experience. As a child, my early-morning chore was to go to Grandma, who was bedridden by a "shock," and stand quietly by her gaping mouth—her teeth grinning from the water glass on the bedside table—to see if her slow, shallow breathing made the covers rise and fall, a motion so subtle it took me a while to be sure they had moved. Sometimes I held my hand over the black hole of her mouth to see if I could feel her slow breathing. Several times I stuck a finger in her mouth, and once when I did it she woke, catching me and grinning, knowing the game.

I was told that no one had expected me to survive a sickly childhood, that I had been in a coma for almost a week when I was five years old. I still remember the hallucinations that came with fever. I was taught that I had survived bronchitis, flu, measles (regular and German), whooping cough, and asthma only because of the prayers of the congregation where my father was deacon. I imagined those prayers rising from Tremont Temple as a great cloudlike pillow, myself perched on the top.

As a paratrooper in World War II, I dealt with the terror of infantry combat by deciding I would die, which pushed back the fear of dying. If I was going to die, then there was no reason to worry about it as I moved through fields and along roads littered with the swollen bodies of the newly dead, friend and enemy alike wearing an expression of surprise.

Minnie Mae has her own history of illness—in a Christian Science home—and loss, as during the war Larry, her nephew, fell ill and died in a matter of days. She knows as well as I do that what can't happen can.

And yet when we get home, we don't go straight to the hospital. (I don't know that years later Minnie Mae will still weep at the memory of the kitchen cleaned by Lee the night before she was taken to the hospital, although she was sick with fever.) Anne and Hannah told us, when we called from the highway, that there was nothing we could do at the hospital. Lee's condition was stable. She was being treated for a high fever. The staff knew what to do, and she would be fine. Lee needed to rest, not to see distraught parents rushing in late at night. That would scare her. And it was after visiting hours, as if that mattered. So we sleep a fitful sleep and in the morning stop at McDonald's for a gulped-down breakfast before we go to our daughter's side.

Her sisters have arrived ahead of us, and Lee is awake, sweating, fever-blurred, but happy to see us, comforted by our presence. Then Dr. Tucker, not hiding his worry, tells us she is being transferred to Massachusetts General Hospital. I don't notice whether he tells us he suspects Reye's syndrome, but he believes this is the cause and thinks the transfer will give her a chance at life. We take turns standing by Lee's bed as we wait for her to be taken to the ambulance. Lee, not knowing it will be the last time she speaks to us, keeps telling us how wonderful her sisters have been, how well they have taken care of her.

6. Tuesday: Shock

We follow the ambulance taking Lee to Massachusetts General Hospital. Dr. Tucker cancels all his appointments and rides to Boston at Lee's side. We are still unable to fully understand why she needs the special care only available in a great medical complex, but we're glad such a place is nearby. The ambulance carrying my daughter to where she will be saved slows, sometimes stops. I can't believe it. The traffic doesn't part or slow at the command of the siren. Filled with a sudden anger, I curse the drivers who don't care that our daughter is so sick she has to get to a Boston hospital right now. Immediately. Sooner than possible. Even as I rant I know that my anger comes from my guilt. Why did we sleep at home last night? Why did we stop for breakfast? Why were we in Vermont when she got sick?

Enough. This is no time to worry about the past. Live in the moment as I did in combat, I tell myself. Get to the hospital. Do what we have to do there. I have to be strong for Lee, for Minnie Mae, for Anne and Hannah, who are driving down in our other car, and for Paul, who will meet us at the hospital. They will visit Lee and then when the doctors figure out what is wrong with her and begin the treatment to cure her, everyone can leave and get on with their lives.

Already we have begun our natural pattern: Minnie Mae prepares herself for the worst by believing the worst will happen, and I, who always try to see the half-empty glass half full, force myself to be hopeful. I am certain they will cure her, we will soon be taking her home, per-haps tonight or the next morning. Then I, the storyteller, will tell everyone of our trip down from Vermont and to the hospital with Lee, how wonderfully kind and skillful the doctors were in caring for her, how in another time we would have lost her but not now, not in 1977.

We see Lee as she is wheeled into pediatric intensive care, where they are best trained to help her. She is asleep. She looks peaceful and free of pain. We find the small waiting room, crowded with the four of us, almost filled when Paul rushes in after getting our call. Later when I lie on the floor to sleep, I take all the floor space. Pediatric intensive care is filled with desperately sick children, some from other parts of the world, but only once in the days ahead will the waiting room be full.

We wait ... and wait and wait, talking less and less, retreating into our own memories and fears until Dr. Shannon, head of pediatric intensive care, finally comes and sits with us. The fact that he sits, listens, explains calmly and quietly, is both comforting and terrifying. It means this is serious. He tells us that Dr. Tucker's diagnosis of Reye's syndrome was brilliant. Supposedly only young children suffer from that disease, but Dr. Shannon knows that many adults develop Reye's syndrome, though they are rarely diagnosed. Because of Dr. Tucker's diagnosis, this is precisely the right place for her, and she will be kept in pediatric intensive care, although she is twenty years old, because they have the expertise to treat her.

Slowly, patiently, knowing it will take us hours, perhaps days to comprehend what has happened, he tells us about Reye's syndrome, a disease I have never heard of. Even the experts really don't know much. Reye's seems to occur after a viral illness, especially when an aspirin has been taken for a fever, as Lee did. In New Brunswick, Canada, there was an outbreak after trees were sprayed for spruce bud worm disease. In Southeast Asia there was another outbreak when they were spraying for something else.

Reye's attacks many organs throughout the body, especially the liver and the brain. Lee's ammonia count is incredibly high. She is in a coma.

Eighty percent of the victims rise from their sickbeds after the crisis passes and are normal, going home to play their oboes, eat submarine sandwiches, return to school, tell the story of their medical adventure, making it amusing so the listeners will laugh.

And the other 20 percent? A flat brain wave.

Lee is terribly sick, but they will do all they can. And as my family and the doctor waited for the crisis to pass during my childhood illnesses, the specialists in this modern hospital will take an old-fashioned lesson in waiting— and we will wait with them.

And then we face some unexpected realities. We are

questioned by other doctors—and eventually by experts from the Centers for Disease Control in Atlanta. They interview Anne and Hannah to document Lee's symptoms, what medication she took, sprays she may have used at the restaurant where she's been waiting on tables for the summer, wasp sprays in our garage. They seem to know as little as we do. We hear rumors of phone consultations—St. Louis, or was it Kansas City? And they question us again and again, together and separately, asking the questions that should not have to be answered by sisters and a boyfriend in front of parents. What drugs, if any, has she used? How sexually active has she been?

And I have an unexpected thought. If Lee dies a virgin, how sad it will be that this loving, caring, sensitive woman dies without experiencing what has been so central to her mother's and my loving and living. Later I discover Minnie Mae feels the same way.

Each time the doctors leave we sit in stunned silence, each of us trying to absorb in our own way what is happening. I feel as if I'm being held out of time, living some impossible nightmare. Surely we will wake and laugh at what we have been dreaming. But it is real, and it becomes clear that we will not know for days if she will be

one of those who get up and walk away or one of the few
whose brain waves run flat.

We take a room in the hotel next door and force each
other to eat something, to shower, to nap, some of us always staying in the waiting room in case there is news.
There is never any question that we will all stay close to
her as long as necessary. There is no going back to work,
no stepping out of this unreal reality and rejoining the
world that flows on around us. We will be here, together.

We take turns to go alone and visit Lee. The smell of
ammonia is strong—her readings are critically high. And
in the middle of all this cold technology is our beautiful
Lee, eyes closed, no sign of pain, peaceful, still alive.

I tell her we are all here with her. Mother. Anne. Hannah. Paul. I explain that the best doctors, nurses, technicians in the world are caring for her.

I tell her we love her.

I tell her to fight.

And I stand in a long silence.

Slowly, carefully, so I won't interfere with the machines
that are keeping her alive, I touch her hand. Then I turn
and leave, as lonely and helpless as I have ever been.

7. Wednesday: Doubt

As it did in combat, my world grows small. The waiting room contains our east, west, north, south. We have asked that no friends come and visit us. We know from previous hospital stays that we would feel the need to entertain, and we do not have the energy or the interest. Our focus is entirely on Lee—and one another.

Paul's parents did come by but did not stay long. Our friends understand and most have stayed away, although I know they want to hold us, comfort us, share this experience of a sick child that so terrifies all who are parents. We phoned a close friend, Stephanie Bradley-Swift, who is the English Department administrative assistant, and she's been calling other friends who, in turn, have been keeping others informed. Our news is mostly no news. We're aware of the support of friends outside of the hospital, feel their concern and their caring, but our focus is on the young woman attached to machines in intensive care down the hall.

We mostly sit in silence. All that needs to be said has been said again and again and again. When we speak it is often in code, a quick reference to what was said before, and a nod of understanding.

Footsteps. Soft footsteps we have become trained to hear. Nurses' and doctors' crepe-soled shoes. Steps starting down the corridor. Stopping at the waiting room. No, starting again. Turning a corner. Silence. Coming closer, closer, closer, passing by.

No news is not good news, not bad news, just not news. Nothing. We are waiting for the crisis to pass, but unspoken is our feeling that the longer it takes, the more damage that is taking place. Reye's syndrome, not modern medicine, is in charge. Nature has to take its slow course, kind or cruel.

I am reporter to my daughter's illness, perhaps to her dying. As a child in an uncomfortable family full of tension and silence, I became a watcher early on. I can remember mysterious and frightening scenes in a flat we left when I was just four—my father's silent leaving and, weeks later, his silent return. I recorded those scenes so filled with silence and messages delivered by looks, gestures, and turning away. It was the ideal childhood for a writer. I know that my training as a reporter began before I could even read the paper. And at fifty-two I have had years of professional training at observation.

I cannot stop myself from taking notes, but I feel guilty. This is not the time for objective reporting, for recording the specific image of the old-fashioned gauge drilled into Lee's skull; to store away the loneliness of the families in the hospital cafeteria late at night, how they try to lift food to their mouths, how they try to start conversations and fail; to measure the distance between Anne and Hannah and note how differently they are responding to this crisis; to document Minnie Mae's quick aging; to wonder how the doctors can handle their obvious stress and caring; to be aware of the distance I am keeping from Minnie Mae, Anne, Hannah, Paul, knowing in some prehistoric way that I have to allow myself some emotional room to do what a father might need to do.

I prowl the hospital I have known since I had memory. I stand under the Bulfinch dome where a dentist, William Thomas Green Morton, demonstrated in 1846 that ether vapor could be used as an effective anesthetic, and I take great comfort in the many medical developments that began or were tested in this medical center. Surely they will find a way to save Lee.

When I cannot take it anymore, I make myself return to combat. When we were under shellfire and I could do nothing but wait it out, I often made myself go to sleep. Three times I was given the last rites in the mistaken belief that I was Roman Catholic, since my name was Murray, and since I was so peacefully sleeping through the shellfire I must be dead.

Now I lay myself down on the cold tile and sleep.

The MGH complex is a jumble of old and new buildings slammed up against an old jail with great gray stone walls in the West End of Boston, where I lived as a young reporter. It is gleaming-new, shabby, drab, dark, or bright, depending on which building you are in. Private patients are stored out of sight of the corridors that have long lines of clinic patients waiting their turn for cheaper care. Hallways are often filled with carts or medical machines, used and then shoved haphazardly where they can be grabbed and rushed to where they are needed next. Technicians and nurses bustle by while doctors stroll, giving off an illusion of calm, certain knowing.

For a while I sit quietly in a waiting room chair, then suddenly get up. I have to get away, to walk. I pass through the always busy emergency department, which I came to so often as a police reporter after a shooting, fire, explosion, or automobile accident. Was it here, as we rushed a gurney to surgery, that a doctor asked me, a young reporter, to hold the gray pudding of a brain where the skull had been shot away? Later I found my father in MGH's emergency room each time I was called in New Hampshire with the news of yet another heart attack. It was in MGH that my father asked me when he was still under the influence of anesthesia if I had lowered the awning on the clothing store Murray & Son, the dream that never was to be but which he couldn't forget. I would carry on a conversation about it as if I was at least here, the compliant son.

"The awning is down, Dad."

"Good, son. Any customers coming down the street?"

"Not yet. I'll get the new sale sign in the window."

"You do that, son."

And it was in a room at MGH that he woke after a biopsy and asked the question I feared: "Is it cancer, son?"

And I firmly answered, "Yes."

My father was a hypochondriac all his life, taking to bed with illnesses real and imagined. He was in the retail business, dealing with women's fashions, and when his buying didn't match his customer's purchasing, he would take to his bed. When my father lost his own store when I was very young, and as he moved from department store to department store to chain store on a long downward slope, he spent days in bed with what was whispered to be a nervous breakdown.

When age made his illnesses real, he was heroic. He had been in training for this role all his life. He was the king of the ward. Mother always wanted a private room, but he wanted to be where he could take charge, alerting nurses—and sometimes doctors—to other patients' needs while carrying on an informal ministry with other patients. He'd wanted to become a minister, but his father took him out of school and sent him to work on his fourteenth birthday. In retirement he ran a senior citizens' religious program at Tremont Temple Baptist Church, where he had been a deacon. A hospital ward gave him a captive audience.

It was also in MGH where the doctors wanted to keep my mother from visiting him. As soon as she arrived, all the beepers and monitors and gauges sounded off, documenting the tension in their marriage, which I had observed from birth.

It was also in this hospital that I sat on a green leather couch in a consulting room and discussed removing extraordinary means in order to give him the gift he wanted: death. The wise young doctor had said they would hook him up to a pacemaker but do nothing else. If he wanted to live ...

Later I saw him wheeled past me in the corridor, asleep with a serene look on his face and the pacemaker resting on his chest. I would never see him alive again.

Years later I came down from New Hampshire to go out for a gluttonous Italian dinner in the North End with Leonard Wheildon the night before he was to enter MGH, where they would remove the cancer and enough of his insides so that he would never be able to eat such a dinner again.

Leonard, a fellow editorial writer on the *Boston Herald*,

was one of the kindest, gentlest men I have ever known. He was empathetic, thoughtful, and always avoided causing others pain, but it was on one of the fancy floors of the hospital in a private room where I came for a last visit that he angrily flung back the covers to show me where they had amputated his manhood. The cancer had reached his brain as well, and he cursed me for having the equipment that had been so cruelly taken from him.

As Lee lies sick unto death, I wonder if the stern fundamentalist faith of my childhood, so long ago rejected, will return. Will I feel a need for prayer? Will I pray? Will I feel a hunger for belief?

I do not. Death is to me final. No heaven, no hell, just a black emptiness without escape.

There is no reason in what has happened to Lee. No God ordained this; no God can save her.

The steps coming down the corridor continue to our door and stop. We all turn to Dr. Shannon, reading the expression on his face, his body language. No good news. We know that before he speaks. And no final bad news. Lee is not dead. Again, the news is essentially no news. The crisis has not arrived and cannot pass until it does. I remember the reproduction of a large painting I have seen many times. There is a large bed with a small child in it. A doctor, formally dressed, leans toward the child; at the foot of the bed is the family, waiting with the doctor for the crisis to pass.

One of us notes it is only Wednesday. It was only Monday when we got the phone call, only Tuesday when we followed the ambulance to MGH to begin the wait that can be measured in hours yet seems like forever. Our optimism begins to fade. Don Graves, our close friend who is also an ordained Presbyterian minister, arrives at the hospital; when Anne tells him that she knows Lee is going to die, they take a long walk.

I feel a great weariness, as if we are being pressed down by a great weight. Numbness blunts each sense, forcing us all to the kind of soldiering on that I did in combat, marching half asleep, going through the motions of living but, in that case, dangerously unaware of the world around us. I taste a bitter, metallic flavor in me that no trip to the water cooler can erase. And the silence when we are beyond talk.

At times I sense that we are moving slowly away from each other, then closer together, floating back and forth in some heavy transparent fluid that makes each moment slow. Anne withdraws into herself, her face dark with grieving and fear. Minnie Mae grows quiet in a terrible, despairing patience that is without hope. Hannah gets up and goes to see someone, to ask a question, to find out, observe. Paul is just Paul, a caring, sweet young man, a scientist who cannot, will not apply reason to what has happened. And her father? I am the writer, trying not to observe, record, write this dreadful narrative in silent phrases, lines, sentences, trying not to tell myself the story of my daughter's dying.

We do not know if it is morning or night. There is no weather in our world. We each go alone to stand by Lee. I cannot believe how alive she looks, so beautiful, so peaceful, so unaffected by the medical war the doctors, technicians, nurses are fighting in her body. But we do not visit her often or stay with her long. We believe she is in the care of doctors and machines, that we have handed her over to professionals and it is our duty not to interfere. Years after it is all over, living backward, I will hate our

discipline, our tearless waiting, our Anglo-Saxon bravery, the stiff upper lip and, worst of all, our leaving her
alone, not touching her, not holding her hand, not talking to her. Years after, I will know that she might have
heard us, might not have spent her last days so terribly
alone in the care of machines.

8. Thursday: Despair

Only in retrospect will I be able to slice our time in the hospital into days. Hours will never be possible. If there is a window in the waiting room, I don't notice it. We don't know if it is morning or night, late or early. We just wait ... wait ... wait while time flows around us.

We sleepwalk our way from waiting room to bathroom and back, waiting room to cafeteria and back, waiting room to hotel shower and back, so tired we stagger, our tongues large and furry in our mouths, our eyes raw and red, our brains going in two directions—maintaining hope and preparing for the end of hope.

Time slows, almost stops.

"He was going to come back and talk to us in an hour."

"It's, let's see, that was twelve minutes ago."

"Seems like an hour."

"Seems like forever."

Specialists are called and consulted. The doctors and residents and interns and nurses and technicians come and go shift after shift, but each time one of us goes to stand by Lee, she is the same. A great battle is being fought in her body, but her face never shows any pain or suffering. At first her peacefulness was a comfort; now it has become frightening. Pain, fear, hurt, terror would all mean she is there. I feel disloyal but hope for her to suffer, to be alive to her dying.

Words and phrases creep along the edges of my skull. "Death." "Vegetable." "Hopeless." "Brain-dead." "Remove extraordinary means." "Pull the plug." "Gift of death." "Brain damage." "Let her go." "Permanent coma." I avoid each one, but they keep passing through my brain.

We begin to talk to ourselves, and once in a while out loud, soft, fragmentary conversations, half finished.

"I had a friend whose daughter after a diving accident lost her sense of humor. . . . Lee would hate a wheelchair. . . . We might be lucky to have a wheelchair. . . . I can't imagine Lee just lying there forever. . . . What if she has to learn to walk … to talk … to think … she could have amnesia, forget who Paul is, who we are …"

We all pause to listen when footsteps come near. Sometimes they stop and a doctor tells us there has been no change. But, we begin to understand that no change is a change for the worse. A crisis has to arrive in order to pass, to release her from the guerrilla disease that holds her captive.

The doctors seem as inarticulate as we are, as if her case has stripped them of the clichéd phrases that worked with others. We try to find comfort in "At least she isn't suffering," "She wants to live," "Lee's a fighter," "This is the best hospital in the world," but none gives us peace.

The father-in-law of Dr. David Ellis, vice president for academic affairs at the university and a friend, drops by. He is an MIT professor and a member of the board of trustees of the hospital, and he assures us everything is being done that can be done.

One at a time we stand in the corridor where the doctors will have to pass by. With words, a gesture, a look, they tell us time after time that there is no change.

Paul is Catholic, and I ask him if he wants to go down

to the chapel at Massachusetts General Hospital for the evening mass. He does, and I go with him. The pews are filled with the halt and the lame, the deformed and the defaced, and the family members of those who have died, are dying, or might soon die.

A boy priest appears to celebrate mass in an unsure voice, but then, when he begins the sermon, his voice grows stronger, more certain. Whatever is happening to the individuals in the congregation or their loved ones is happening because of God's will. He has a purpose and we should take comfort in that.

Paul suddenly rises and storms out. I chase after him. He will not belong to a church, he says, that preaches such a message; he will not believe in a God that can make lively Lee be so still, so unaware, so near death at twenty.

I force Paul to leave the hospital with me and walk. We circle the block as he rages against the priest, against the Roman Catholic religion, against all religions, against God. I agree but urge him to wait before making a decision. His father went to seminary but left before taking vows. His family, however, has made two deep rivers of belief flow together: his father's French Canadian Catholic faith and his mother's Irish Catholic tradition. I urge him to delay a decision that would so hurt his family. At last he agrees and we go back to our waiting.

Sometimes one of us will try to bring Lee into the waiting room alive, laughing, by telling the same stories over and over again: how much she likes sub sandwiches, the time she tossed the six-pack of beer out of our Chevy Suburban toward a police car, what she and Anne have been planning to do to the apartment they have rented in Cambridge, how much she worried about the beggars we saw in Tijuana, how much she likes her new oboe, what she will be studying at the conservatory. But we do this less and less.

One time Minnie Mae and I are in the hotel room and she says, "Lee is going to die," and I rage at her: "Don't give up. We have to hope." I yell and attack, and the madder I become, the more she knows and I know that she is right.

I don't know how we creep toward the subject, but Paul leans forward, the anguish on his face.

"One of our classmates was in the front seat of a Volkswagen van in a head-on accident. He was horribly crushed.

They kept him alive in a coma. We told each other that we didn't want that. We wanted him to be let go."

Later, "Did you ever discuss burial or cremation?"

"Lee wanted to be cremated."

Awkwardly, hesitantly, I tell them of my burial nightmares after my father died. We all talk around the subject. Everyone prefers cremation. Then we sit back, not looking at each other, feeling we are traitors to Lee, who lies close by, still alive.

We all know we have passed from hope to despair. We are preparing ourselves for the inevitable, hoping, hoping, hoping it won't be inevitable, but feeling that it will be. There has been no change, and no change means. . . .

Stephanie Bradley-Swift and her husband, Dan Swift, break our rule and come to visit us this evening. I am immediately angry, and then I make myself calm. Anger has become a constant companion the longer we wait, and it needs a target. But Steph is the friend we called who has been relaying the messages of no change to friends who, in turn, have called other friends. We have, however, been waiting too long for talk. We allow Steph and Dan to enter our silence, and we feel their concern.

I go back to stand by Lee, no longer speaking, just being there. I see no suffering, no pain, nothing. Not an eyelid flutter if I speak, no answering movement if I hold her hand. The nurses and the doctors are careful not to reveal what they know, and in doing that they reveal everything.

9. Friday: Letting Go

When I shave Friday morning the face in the mirror wears the mask I have not seen in thirty-two years, since our last battle across the Rhine in Germany was over and we moved to the rear. In the waiting room I see the same expression—sunken eyes, drawn skin, and a dumb expression of disbelief—on the faces of Minnie Mae, Anne, Hannah, and Paul. The faces reflect an exhaustion of the body, the emotions, the spirit. What can't have happened has, and our brains are numbed by a reality we know we will have to accept but cannot yet. We no longer feel hope but irrational denial.

Each day we have been functioning as animals, surviving the moment, washing, forcing food, napping, pacing, trying to reach out from our private hells to others and failing. All there was to be said has been spoken again and again; all that could be imagined has been. There is nothing more to say, nothing we can do. We sit in this too-familiar small waiting room in a silence as heavy and dark as black snow.

Then a nurse who has been caring for Lee all night bursts into the waiting room, angry and distraught, and attacks us for not spending more time with Lee. We don't understand what she is saying at first. Then we realize that she is attacking us for our lack of loving care, and we shrink within ourselves.

We want to be at her side, but we are not the kind of family that we shared the hospital waiting room with for a few hours, weeping and wailing. We are of the stiff-upper-lip tradition. It is weakness to cry, strength to show as little emotion as possible. We screw our feelings down tight. And we do not want to get in the way of the doctors, nurses, and technicians who are fighting to keep her alive.

Now we feel instantly guilty. Of course we visit, but now—too late—we know we should have stayed at her side. The nurse attacks over and over again, stabbing us with guilt. We didn't know. We didn't want to get in the way. Are we weak, scared, thoughtless, unloving?

The nurse finishes her rage, swirls out of the room. The care has been wonderful. Early on I asked Dr. Shannon how he and the others could be so involved with Lee, so caring about all their patients. How did they handle it? He told me he played the piano, that was his release. But now this nurse . . .

My guilt becomes anger, and I storm off to complain. I am told she is frustrated at how little she can do for Lee. She shouldn't have spoken to us the way she did, but they are all concerned, helpless, and the anger has to go somewhere.

Later I will realize I should have known what this means, but right now I don't. Or I do and am denying it. I check on everyone like a mother hen. How's Paul doing? Anne? Hannah? Minnie Mae? Myself? I can feel that small waiting room close in on me now. A world shrunken to a room. One door. That is where we will get the news. Each time Dr. Shannon comes through the door to sit with us, we wonder if this is the time, but he quickly makes it clear there is no news, good or bad. Until one time late in the morning.

He starts by explaining how the nurse who attacked us felt and why. It is frustrating to her to be able to do nothing. That I understand. Nothing can be done. Nothing will be done. Every option has been tried and has failed. This entire medical center can do nothing. The words fly past me, but the message is clear. The electrical waves coming from Lee's brain are flat. I try to make myself cold, drawing on what I learned in combat: how to go beyond feelings to duty.

This whole week has been an exercise in denial followed by acceptance. From the first phone call we have tried to deny what has been happening while accepting what our brains and hearts can process. When I supervised first- and second-year writing courses at the University of New Hampshire, a very wise graduate student, now Dr. Donna Rubin, a professor of English at Salem State University, wrote a dissertation that documented that most composition students learned skills in the first semester that they were only able to practice in the next semester. She found that there was a significant delay between learning and performance. It has been the same way with us. It has taken us time to accept what we already knew and act upon it. I do not understand much of what Dr. Shannon is saying, but I get the message. Lee cannot live without machines, and even with them she cannot smile, think, imagine, communicate, hear, speak, see, touch, taste, weep, laugh, love.

It is Hannah who says what has to be said. There is no choice. We have to release Lee from the nonlife that the machines are giving her. We will give our daughter the gift of death.

As her father, I speak to the doctor alone in the corridor, ask again if there is any hope, even the slightest hope, any experimental treatment that can be tried. At the end of our conversation he answers with silence, and I see a resident with whom we have become friendly rush by, her face wet with tears.

I give him our consent, allowing the formal letting go, as I did with Father. Mother. Now daughter. The ultimate gift of love: death.

I return to the waiting room and we all, each terribly alone, visit Lee for the last time.

I am last, and beside the aloneness, an arctic land-scape without horizons, I feel helpless. It is the job of a man, a father, to solve problems, to protect his family. I have not, I cannot. I was not even there when she got sick; instead I reassured myself I was earning her tuition money. I did not rush to her side but slept at home, went to McDonald's for breakfast. I went with her to a great medical center, but I did not spend the hours, the days since then at her side. All the wires, tubes, monitors, all the doctors, specialists, nurses, technicians can do noth-ing. I say goodbye, tell her how much we love her, hoping there is a chance she can hear, then turn on my heel to march into the corridor and live the scene I will in the future dream so often.

I call information and get the number of the only fu-neral home I can remember, the one that took care of a colleague who committed suicide. Waiting for the call to be answered, I feel old and very cold. On the earlier occasion, a state trooper came to the hospital and took charge. My colleague was divorced. Her former hus-band had been called and was on his way from a dis-tant city. So was her lover. Her father had been located but would not come to her side. We could not find her mother.

The state police officer slammed down the telephone when another colleague demanded that no man, neither ex-husband or father, make any decision about her and then asked that her unfinished manuscript be given to her immediately.

He gave me a look of disbelief that quickly turned to command. "Call your department," he said. "Seal her office."

I did, and then the state trooper received another call. Another woman friend was demanding thousands of dollars she said was owed her—and my colleague not yet dead. He hung up the phone and turned to me. "You are next of kin."

"Can you do that?" I asked.

"I just did."

I went with him to the doctor and said, "Let her go."

"Is he next of kin?" the doctor asked.

"He is now," said the trooper.

The funeral director who had taken care of that colleague when we let her go remembers me.

"Where is your daughter?"

"At Mass General. In Boston."

"We'll take care of her."

"Cremation," I hear myself say. An image of fire fills my brain.

I walk back to my family in the waiting room, and Hannah says, "Let's go home."

Survival

10. Home Without Lee

It is late afternoon of the day we let Lee go and I am at home, sitting in the green chair in the living room. I have done my cruel duty as a father and a man. I feel like an empty bag of skin, drained of blood, bones, anything. Empty beyond sadness, beyond strength, obligation, responsibility.

Soon I will have to start with the "arrangements." I have been concerned with Minnie Mae. Anne. Hannah. Paul. Now it is my time. I will withdraw from life, crawl into myself. Then the doorbell rings. I cannot see anybody, will not see anyone. I hear voices and know it is the Heilbronners, old friends and neighbors, but today I cannot face their aggressive caring. Someone else lets them in. Hans shouts, "We have brought food." I hear them in the kitchen. I do not move from my green chair to thank them. The idea of food makes my stomach turn. I will never eat again.

Then Phyllis is kneeling on the floor beside my chair feeding me. I have no choice. The food comes up to my mouth. I cannot turn away from this attack of love and concern. I cannot spit out what they have made for us. I open my mouth. One mouthful I swallow. Another. And another. I take the plate and feed myself. I will eat. I will live.

We do not belong to a church or temple, we have no religious traditions to guide us with the arrangements, and we have no ethnic rituals, only the Scots tradition of the stiff upper lip in my case and the German heritage of no tears, emotions under control, in Minnie Mae's case.

I break tradition. I wept at the hospital. I weep now. No apology. I weep in public and private. I will not keep my grief locked up inside me, as my mother's family always has. My father was a weeper and was ridiculed by his wife's family for showing emotion. I will be the father I have tried to escape since childhood, fearing his weakness was passed down to me. Well, it is time to weep, and I will cry openly, without shame.

Unlike my father, who had no childhood, played no sports, and felt unmanly because he had missed his war, I have played sports and served as a paratrooper under fire. My testosterone rating is high enough on the manliness scale. If anyone has a problem with my weeping, tough.

Minnie Mae will not weep until fifteen or more years later, when a sociology student interviews her about grieving. But today I know, and Anne and Hannah know, how deep her grief is. Silently, not showing it, she grieves just as much as I do. If people do not like her not weeping, shove it. We will mourn in our own way, I tell Anne and Hannah. We will do what we have to do to survive, not worry if anyone approves or not.

Hannah was in the chorus of *The Sound of Music* at a local playhouse when Lee took sick. She will go on tonight, and we will go to see her even if it is the day Lee died. Lee would want us to, and so we go. I don't know if our friends and neighbors will disapprove—and I don't care. We will grieve in our own way. We will celebrate Lee with an evening of music. It will be right for us.

During intermission I see myself, as if I were a stranger, walk over to a young man horribly tortured by cerebral palsy or some such illness of the nervous system and start talking with him. I find myself unexpectedly at ease with his random movements, his difficult speech. During the second act I realize I have been changed by Lee's death. And it is not all bad. Lee would have approved of this reaching out.

It will not, however, be easy. I have to learn how to live this changed life. When I wake the next morning, I lie paralyzed with the weight of the last week and the long future without Lee. What do I do? There are no choices. Suicide? That would not help Minnie Mae, Anne, Hannah. Flee? Take off? I must—want to—hold Minnie Mae, Anne, Hannah closer than ever. Climb into a bottle of sour mash bourbon? I started down that road once. Not again. There are no choices, no escape.

I give myself a command to swing my feet over the edge of the bed as a pendulum that will help force my torso upright. Sit to guard against vertigo. Put one foot ahead of the other and go to the bathroom. Wash my face. Go downstairs. Pour grapefruit juice. Take pills. And then what?

It is a day of decisions, a day for the "arrangements"— the term I have seen in so many obituaries, including those I wrote. That is another task. I will have to write an obit. Someone will.

The small, painful tasks are what will save us, I tell myself, almost believing it. Baby steps. Stunned, not yet accepting what has happened, exhausted from the waiting, flannel-mouthed, eyes burning, we make decisions.

Reverend Snow calls. His daughters are friends of our daughters. We can use his Episcopal church; he doesn't need to do the service or even be there. We say thanks and decide there will be no formal funeral, just a graveside service. We are wiped out from this week's waiting. My mother and father are dead, but if we invite Minnie Mae's mother and aunt who live in Washington, D.C., we will have to care for them, and they are elderly and not easy to deal with.

Their reactions to the news of Lee's death makes our decision easier than it might have been. When we phone Katie, Minnie Mae's mother, with our dreadful news, she says only, "How could God have done this to me?" Not then or later does she offer one word of sympathy for her daughter. Aunt Lillie, as always, tops Katie: "I don't know how you can burn her up and stick her in the ground."

I do not realize how little family support we have;

that will come later. Now we do not expect it. Both of us, from an early age on, felt more responsibility for our parents than they did for us. Minnie Mae's brother, who is six years older and lives in Connecticut, has been distant since high school and college. I am an only child. In many such stories there is a great sweeping in of relatives to be with the family, to comfort them, to help with arrangements, to share their loss. But it is not so for us.

Our neighbors, though, give us more support than we know. We haven't yet realized it, but they too had a telephone tree that passed the word from the hospital all over town. Now that we are home, neighbors drop by with food but, more important, they listen to our story over and over and over again, somehow realizing we have to tell them each detail so that sometime in the future we can accept this story of loss, which until now has always been somebody else's.

It must be awful for them, but we tell the story of Lee's dying in brutal detail to each of them. Some must have heard it twice, three times, more. I listen to Minnie Mae's telling and then do my own telling, always surprising myself by the flood of details that cannot be dammed. Narrative is a human necessity.

What we will not know until later is that all the visits have been carefully orchestrated so that we are never too long alone and never have more than one visit at a time. The Heilbronners, Lindens, Graves, Clarks, Ladds, Swifts, and so many others. Andy Merton and Gail Kelly, students who have become colleagues. Colie Hogan, an industrialist for whom I ghostwrote—we are not close, but he lost a son in Vietnam and knows the territory. Our friends, neighbors, colleagues become family to us, perhaps a far more thoughtful family than real relatives would have been. It will take me some time to realize how they sensed our need and answered it, listened and cared.

There are times, however, when I can no longer bear our obsessive telling. I walk out of the house, trying to walk away from the story of Lee's dying and my own telling of it. When no one is visiting, Minnie Mae and I start compulsively telling again—and yet again—the too-familiar story to each other. When I cannot bear to hear another line of Minnie Mae's story, I talk right over her about the Red Sox and she stops, understanding my need to escape. When she cannot bear to hear another of my tellings, she stops me in midsentence and I understand.

I do not really know what Anne and Hannah are doing

as they return to their friends. I know they have been there for us and we for them. I know they have been consulted about each decision and made many of them. We arranged for cremation after the conversation in the waiting room at Mass General. We are not invited to attend that burning, although I have heard of people who go. We do not.

Later I will not be able to entirely penetrate the walls I have already started to build around this week; I will only be able to zoom in on certain moments. I call Mr. Wilcox, who is in charge of the Durham cemetery. He is a dignified old Yankee whose wife was one of Anne and Lee's high school English teachers and the town historian. He has always kept his distance, but now, with great dignity and an unexpected caring, he walks the cemetery with us, showing us which lots are available. As we walk through the rows of headstones I am somehow comforted by the number of familiar names I see there. Lee—and we in our time—will lie with neighbors.

We have never been much for cemeteries, scoffing privately when we visit Minnie Mae's mother in Kentucky and make the obligatory visit to the cemetery. We do not visit my parents' graves. They do not stay in their graves anyway but keep showing up in dreams, thoughts, memories, conversations. They are not in the ground but alive in us. Now we will have a daughter lying here. I will never again feel about cemeteries as I did before Lee's dying, but will we visit often? I don't know.

The bright August day seems unreal. As we walk over the uneven grass, my feet remember when, as a teenager, I returned home after an appendix operation and before going up to our flat left the cement walkway and stepped out on the grass to celebrate my recovery, my new life. And Lee would have done the same, if . . .

I force myself to chat, to keep a stiff upper lip, to be a man, but I cannot believe we are picking out a cemetery lot. Perhaps in old age we would do that to help our children, but that would be, should be years away. My grandmothers both died at eighty-nine, my father at seventy-nine, Mother at eighty-two, Minnie Mae's mother at ninety-six. But now we are going to bury a daughter ahead of us. At twenty. Only twenty.

Anne and Hannah suggest the gravestone should be the flat, slightly tipped stone from our rock wall where the girls had tea parties and, later, picnic meals we didn't even know about. We ask someone at the cemetery whom could we get to move the stone, and right away, it seems, a town front-loader is at the house, is plucking the large stone out of the wall and carrying it to our new burial plot.

The girls want to be sure that Lee's middle name, Emmerich, her mother's maiden name, is on the stone, and when I talk about it with the old gravestone cutter, who has seventy years at his trade, he says, "It's the worst for the mothers, a child going before." And for the fathers, I say to myself. It is against the natural order of life.

The letters start coming in. I was writing a letter of sympathy the morning of the day we got the phone call— is it not a full week yet?—and I remember wondering what I could say and if it made any difference. Now I know it did. We often speak of Karen Mower's letter, the comfort it gives us. All the letters, no matter how well or poorly written, bring us comfort. Many tell of similar losses they or their family suffered, and the message behind the message is that they survived. They went on living, and so will we.

We stop by to see an old friend, Bill Sims, who called. As we were losing Lee, he was having a new baby, Andrea, and when we arrive I am surprised, almost angry,

when he shoves the infant into my arms. And then holding this tiny person, comforting her, making her safe,
protected as I could not protect Lee, gives me an amazing
moment of calm and peace.

The business of death goes on in a blur. We visit the
funeral home, arrange for Social Security and the death
certificate, hear suggestions for memorial services here
and at the University of Massachusetts, decide that if
people want to give money we will figure out later how
best to celebrate her life, and plan the service.

Will our old friend and faculty colleague Don Graves,
who is ordained in the Presbyterian Church, do the service? Of course he will. Will Betty come? Yes. We invite
Paul, his parents and brother. And for Paul, who is Catholic,
we ask Father Joe Desmond, the local priest, to take part
in a burial service for a family of nonbelievers.

As a lapsed Baptist, I am uncomfortable going to the
mysterious Roman Catholic rectory. Father Desmond
immediately agrees to participate, and so begins a long
friendship. We tell the funeral home, and they help us
schedule the service, arrange for the actual burial.

I have been a fan of A. E. Housman since a fellow soldier introduced me to *Shropshire Lad* when I was in the

army, and I once thought of doing a dissertation on him. His "To an Athlete Dying Young" should be read. A poem by Theodore Roethke? An editorial by William Allen White about the death of his daughter? I am not sure. The service blurs, but one thing I see clearly is the gravedigger, standing by his old car, at a proper distance. I didn't know he was a gravedigger, but we have nodded to each other on the sidewalk, and I have often had morning coffee where he does. His standing there is important. Lee will not be buried by a stranger. I look back as we leave the cemetery and see him start slowly toward where he will dig and place the so very small box of ashes.

When we return home from the brief service, we find food from the neighbors, set out while we have been gone. We stay together to eat, to comfort each other, not to be alone, none of us believing that it has been just one week to the day that Lee was taken by ambulance to the hospital.

11. Strange Comfort

I wake the morning after Lee's burial and realize it is the first day of a new life, one I never dreamed I would experience. The day stretches out like a road in Nebraska, long, straight, and without landmarks. What do I do to start this life without Lee?

I make myself remember one simple task, then another and another. As I did yesterday, I swing my legs over the side of our high bed and let them fall, using their weight as a pendulum to help me sit up.

Now I am sitting up, my hands on the edge of the bed frame. What now? I do nothing. I wait until the vertigo passes.

I have to think what comes next. The bathroom. I

push myself from the edge of the bed and walk toward our bathroom, feeling as if I were moving through a river of glue, each step a conscious effort. So this is how my days will be.

I have the comfort of habit, and so I perform the elemental ritual of life, aware of each act, aware that Lee will never again go to the bathroom. I wash my face. She will never feel the waking splash of cold water in the morning. I start to look toward her door at the end of the hall, start to move down the corridor, make myself stop. I cannot keep imagining that life will reverse itself, the clock spinning backward, the torn calendar pages returning to the wall. I turn and make myself walk down the stairs she will never again walk, telling myself I cannot live my life like this. Will I be able to live without remembering Lee trying to learn how to use a spoon each time I touch a spoon, Lee's baby juice cup when I pour juice, Lee sitting with Paul in his car when I hear a car stop and I look out the bedroom window at night? Will I be forever caught in the tangled vines of memory?

I pour my juice, remember that I take pills, and take them. What do I do next? I go up to Young's and buy the papers saved for me. A neighbor I like but hardly know comes up beside me at the magazine rack and says, "My wife backed over our baby, before we came here. We never talk about it."

And they don't talk about it now, but I have a deeper understanding of the flowers he picked himself and unexpectedly brought to Minnie Mae, gardener to gardener, after we came home from the hospital. I realize that now I am a member of a secret or underground society: parents whose children have died.

As I walk home, I keep thinking of the silence in that house, which I pass many times each day—the large but unspoken presence of that baby, all that is avoided, not discussed, kept from each other.

This will not be our way, I decide, probably can't be my way anyway. Minnie Mae is capable of long silence, her way of punishing a husband who can blow up, say what never should be said, and forget it, returning five minutes later to ask, "What's wrong?" I will not tolerate silence, the dreadful unsaids of my childhood. We will talk, telling each other the story of Lee's death until it becomes real. We will not let Lee disappear into a terrible silence. We will talk of what she did that she should not have done, as well as how much it meant to us that she and Paul had decided not to party last New Year's but to share the evening with us, to celebrate their quiet, deep relationship that might last a lifetime. Well, it did. Eight months from that moment was her lifetime. Only eight months and less than a week.

I can, however, understand our neighbors' silence, how mother and father and brothers and sisters cannot talk of such a dreadful accident, how that is one way to survive. But it will not be ours.

I admit now what I have not admitted before: that in combat the memory of my fiancée, who became my first wife, blurred and became unfocused until I looked at the snapshot I carried with me, and then increasingly it seemed a picture of a stranger. I hope Lee will not fade in memory; twenty-five years later I will be able to say that she has not.

I find myself in those first days seeing her, saving something to tell her, guarding her from harm. It has been my occasional habit when waking in the night to patrol the corridor from our bedroom. I need no light in the familiar, shadowed dark and step gently, careful as the infantryman I was. This night I suffer the guilt that I did not protect Lee from the invisible attack of a guerrilla disease whose name I had never heard. So much for the old soldier on guard duty.

Hannah's room on the left. I stand in the shadows until I see her covers gently rise and fall as my grandmother's used to when I performed my childhood chore to see if she had survived the night. In another year she will be off to college. Next door on the left is Anne's. Again I wait for the sheet's rise and fall. Soon she'll be gone as well, perhaps to the apartment in Cambridge she and Lee leased, perhaps somewhere else, but living her life apart from us as she should, returning as a visitor. I think for a moment of my great-grandparents, who sent their children off to a new world knowing they would never see them again— the other side of the great story of emigration. And then, at the end of the corridor, Lee's door. I cannot stop myself; pushing against the emptiness, I force myself inside. The bed is as flat as the hospital bed that morning I returned to the Quincy city hospital and found Mother gone, the mattress stripped of her memory.

I turn and leave this room. The curtain has fallen on the first act. The high drama of the phone call, the rush to wait, the decision to give the gift of death, cremation, and burial is done. Now we must learn how to live again.

We hold on to routine, try to find comfort in the ordinary. Chores, errands, the small habits of our lives. And the busy work of death goes on. Papers to sign, papers to record, the leftover fragments of a life to pick up and put away. Where should contributions to Lee's memory be sent? Where deposited? What would Lee want done? The University of Massachusetts wants to have a memorial service, a concert, something. The mail keeps coming in and the phone continues to ring and people drop by, never too many, but a constant flow of caring. Her high school friends have a memorial service. I sit there stunned, hoping to survive their kindness.

Calls to return, letters to answer, decisions to make—each chore a necessary move toward the reality that Lee is dead. Dead and buried. Paul has gone home with his parents. Betty and Don Graves have left. Just one week has passed.

Minnie Mae and I just look at each other. All has been said that could be said—again and again and again. We have been spoken to in the language of touch—hugs, handshakes, a pat on a shoulder, a hand held. Now alone, we must turn to whatever tasks are at hand, escaping into the familiar ordinariness of our lives.

I try to imagine the future. Will we "get over it" and be cured of mourning? Will we forget and find comfort in forgetting? Will we remain in the unreal reality, dreaming through life, hoping we will wake and it will all be untrue? Then I shop in a store in our small town and the owner, who I have in my grief forgotten has lost a son, shocks me by saying, "It won't get any better, Don."

I step back as if he hit me. He watches me but refuses to apologize or attempt to gentle his brutal counsel, but strangely, as I leave, I find myself taking comfort from that statement. Lee's death will be part of us forever. It will mark us forever. There will be healing as there is when a leg is amputated. We will become who we are: "the Murrays, who lost a daughter, you know." And as we live this life, we will always feel the leg that others cannot see, that invisible leg I have heard amputees talk about that feels cold, pain, itches, lives on in memory.

It will not get any better, and I feel a strange comfort in that. I will have to live this changed life as well as I can. There will be no healing, but I will become familiar with this new life, always having at my side the daughter no one else can see. I might even find it a comfort to know she will always be near.

12. The Tellings

When people ask what happened to Lee, we tell them, compulsively, obsessively, from beginning to end, giving the horrified listeners far more than they want to know. We start with the phone call in Vermont, the trip down, her telling us at the hospital how wonderfully her sisters took care of her, the last thing she told us, the trip down to Boston following the ambulance, how cars didn't get out of the way of the ambulance, how she looked in intensive care, the tubes, wires, meters, the gauges in her skull, how few people were in the tiny waiting room, what we knew about Reye's syndrome, how we each said goodbye alone, how I had to call the funeral home before she was dead.

Once, years before, a doctor gave me a diet pill but did not tell me to avoid alcohol. I had a martini and started to talk. I could not stop. I observed myself talking, tried to stop, and finally went to my third-floor office, where I filed papers, talking away, sort of making sense. I heard myself but could not stop.

It is like that with us. Minnie Mae or I will tell the story again and again to each other, to the same people, on the telephone and in person, to family, friends, even strangers. It will take me a while to realize how necessary this is. It is narrative as much as anything else that gets us through these first weeks, the ancient human need to tell the stories of our lives.

We have to tell and retell the story of Lee's slow dying to convince ourselves that it has happened. It was so unexpected, so quickly serious, her illness so mysterious and hard to understand, that we have to burn the story into our consciousness. The pain is in every telling, searing sharp. It hurts anew, yet it has to be told. It is not comforting, not healing; we do not understand after a telling why this had to happen to our sunny Lee. We just have to make it true by its being told. Lee mysteriously got sick. She got worse. She died. She died.

We have to say the phrases: "Reye's syndrome," "re-move extraordinary means," "wait for the crisis to pass," "flat brain waves." The harder they are to say, the more necessary it seems to say them.

In telling the story, we give an order to the events that they did not seem to have at the time. We follow the chronology but emphasize the crucial moments, intro-duce Dr. Daniel Shannon and the many other doctors. We close off the doubts we had about giving our daughter the gift of death. Our story talks at times about what Paul said she had said about being a vegetable after a friend had a horrible accident, and that she preferred cremation to being buried in the ground.

Gradually the story becomes our reality, but we still have to tell it. It is part of the narrative of our lives and will forever be. When I imagine Lee coming home and walking up the driveway, calling out that it was a joke, slipping into the party through the back door, I tell the story again, using narrative to snuff out hope. This is what happened. This is what is: Lee is dead.

13. Under Neighbors' Eyes

The support of friends and neighbors that was, to me, so unexpected, thoughtful, and kind has become a gentle burden. As I go out in the small world of this college town, I become aware that people are watching me, and at first I resent it. What happened to my family is so profoundly private that I want no pity, no compassion, no support, no curiosity, and certainly no tribute to a bravery that I do not feel. All I did was put one foot in front of the other. We did what had to be done, what all families have to do to deal with a death in the family. I want my grief to be private. Yet people come up and hug me or take my hand, ask me what happened and how we are doing.

I try to respect my neighbors' interest, but I just want to be left alone so I can walk within this dark column of loneliness and loss that each of us feels. Lee is dead. Lee is dead. I have to keep repeating those words, aloud and silently, to make them true.

But I also have to meet their eyes, accept what they have to give, and go on. The walls around me move back. Some color returns to my gray world, and I see that people I hardly know or do not know at all are observing me from the next aisle over in the store, from across the street, in the parking lot from their car, from two tables away in the restaurant.

And then I realize I am observing Minnie Mae, Anne, and Hannah, thinking they do not know I am studying them to see how they are taking it, how they greet their friends, how they look when they do not know I am looking.

For all the changes in our civilization, we still live in villages, in neighborhoods, the small places where we are familiar to others. Our family has passed through one of the most elemental human stories: the loss of a child, the loss of a sister. They are studying us in fear that it might happen to them, with old-fashioned nosiness, with concern, and most of all for instruction.

I have experienced what they most fear. The lightning has struck near them. Not on TV or in the newspaper, not in the story of a friend who has a friend or relative who lost a child, but on the next street, the same department at the university. In our village we learn from each other.

Registering the car, passing in a prescription to the pharmacist, buying bread or cheese, doing business at the post office or bank, attending a meeting and, later, parties, just walking the sidewalk, living our lives, surviving. Our neighbors are asking themselves: "How would I act? How would my partner behave? How would my children survive?"

I do not want this role. In combat I was no hero, just another young man playing the role of soldier, trying to be brave, get the job done, not reveal the terror that must have infected us all. But by hiding it, by joking it away with black humor, we helped each other play the soldier's role.

There is no black humor in the death of a child, but I

realize I have a role to play. It is better to talk than to cover everything with the secrecy so popular in my childhood and the Scots policy of the stiff upper lip. I allow tears to flow if they come, I laugh if it is appropriate, trying to show that such a loss can be survived.

I accept the obligation of role model, one who can strip away some of the mystery about death in a society where we die alone, as Lee did, left to the cold comfort of machines. I will tell her story and mine. I will demonstrate that we can go on.

I often feel I am faking it. I'm not this strong, I'm not this open, I'm not doing this well, but what has so often happened in my life is occurring again. I become the role. I was the scaredy-cat walking brave by the bully, the right tackle playing as if he wasn't afraid of being hurt, the soldier moving against the enemy, the reporter asking the questions that no one should ask, the professor standing before a class as if he knows the subject even though he is learning by teaching it.

I am learning to be brave by acting brave, discovering it is all right to break down—for a moment or two—by breaking down, demonstrating that the uncomfortable question can be answered by answering it.

I hope I do not feel pride that would make the gods test me again, but I am making it. I have experienced the never-spoken-about and can speak of how it feels in that world no one ever plans to explore. In my walk, in my smile, in my ordinariness, I can say, "You could do it if you have to, but I hope you never do."

14. Escape

It is now late August in a New Hampshire town touched by the tide of the Atlantic Ocean. In fact it is not the heat but the humidity. We swelter. The air is heavy even in our pine woods, even when we rise in the morning. It is unusually "close," as the natives say.

And it isn't only the weather that is too close, but the neighbors. We have survived on their sympathy and support, curiosity and caring in the past few weeks, and now we know our family of friends will be there when we need them. But it is time to escape. We need to be alone as a smaller family, four instead of five, to mourn and heal in our own way.

Now as the high drama of sickness and death grows a

few weeks distant, the differences between Anne and Hannah show. The family is smaller, and they are trying to grow closer but not only are at different stages in their lives but are of greatly different personalities. Minnie Mae and I like both personalities and see ourselves and each other in them, but they are dramatically unalike. They try to close the gap left by Lee, but it is not easy.

There is unfinished business. Anne and Lee had planned a picture of the three sisters, but Hannah was busy, and now it is too late. Small matters become large.

Soon Anne will have to move to Cambridge, look for work, begin the life that has been delayed by Lee's death. Hannah will start college and take the writing course at the university that was arranged before. We all mark our life with befores and afters. I pull rank and make sure Hannah will be in Sue Wheeler's class. She is a master teacher who will know how to respond to the efforts Hannah will make to write of Lee's death—and how hard it will be. I will meet my classes, and Minnie Mae will do what she has done for so many years—make our lives easier by her efforts.

In some way I cannot recall, we have decided to go camping as a family, something we have never done before (and, it turns out, will not do again). We head north to Canada, a far enough escape yet near enough to make it there and back before September's school opening. We have previously explored New Brunswick and Nova Scotia, hope someday to go north to Newfoundland and even the edge of Labrador, but there is not time now, and so we head to Prince Edward Island, where we find the perfect geography for healing.

PEI is protected on all sides and does not have the craggy boundaries against an angry North Atlantic that extend from Maine north and which we find so ruggedly beautiful. This island is peaceful, calm, a place of gently rising and falling potato fields, farms and villages, winding roads and long inviting beaches.

We survive one rainstorm in our tents and several sibling and marital storms as the angers and rages related to the death of a sister and daughter break out and subside. What is said has to be said and forgotten. I stop the car in the middle of a road and can see silhouetted figures leaning toward each other, but I cannot hear what was said. I like to believe that we are being healed by this landscape.

I have always imagined another life as an artist, and

one way I deal with my grief is to sketch the quiet landscape in black ink. It is late August, and most days are
sunny and unexpectedly warm for the north country, but
my pen reveals dark woods, bare winter trees, and houses
standing alone in vast fields. I draw house after house,
and it will not be until years later that I see that not one
farmhouse has a single window or door, just line after
line of clapboards allowing no entry or escape.

15. Learning a New Life

Home from camping, Lee in her grave, we each try to find the trail of the lives we led before our world changed. We can no longer deny reality, but we cannot yet accept it. The death of a daughter used to be something that happened on the ten o'clock news, in a newspaper, to a family three streets over whose name you do not know. Not us.

For all the comfort and companionship, there is an enormous loneliness between us and our best friends, even among the four of us. Each loss of Lee—to classmates, old friends, boyfriend, sisters, father and mother—is different. Our Lees were similar but significantly different. There was not one Lee who died, but many.

We were close during her dying, close during the days of preparation for burial, but then Paul went back to live in his loneliness, and when we return from our camping trip, each of each has to reenter his or her own aloneness. Minnie Mae and I spoke frequently in the eleven months between our first meeting and marriage of the importance of our each having lived alone successfully. We felt that boded well for our marriage. We would know, no matter how close our marriage, that we could still be alone. We did not know how much that would be tested by Lee's death.

I feel at times in these first months of our new life that I can measure in precise terms the distance between us. We have to draw close, to reach out, and yet to back off. It is an intricate and individual dance of caring. As mother and father, we have to keep adjusting the distance between us, and then the distance between us and each of our surviving daughters. They have as well to measure the distance between each other, between each of them and each parent, and then each of us has to negotiate the distance between us and Paul, who will, we all know and do not say, leave the family that can no longer be his.

What used to be the familiar routines of our lives now takes effort to remember, and when it is found, it appears alien. What used to seem important often no longer is, and what we took for granted or even passed by without seeing is now significant.

Food is straw, tasteless and choking. Sometimes I stagger as if the surface of the earth is a ship on stormy seas. I was always able to concentrate, but now my mind wanders. It's not just those moments when a word overheard, an image caught at the edge of vision, a few notes played on an oboe, a color, a texture, the perfume of an Italian submarine sandwich brings Lee into the room, alive and laughing, until I make her dead by a terrible force of will. The mind goes numb. Memory shuts down. What did I just say? What did Minnie Mae just say? How does this sentence connect with the last one and lead to the next? What in the world is the television commentator saying? I find a fountain pen in my hand and stare at it. What is this tool intended to do?

Life is a gray-and-white photo, the trees blurred, the road unclear, sea fog on a sunny day. Or life is too clear, sharp-edged, colors so bright they hurt my eyes, everywhere I turn a reminder of life and then the always unexpected realization that Lee is not living, that she cannot not feel grass under her feet, a sheet tucked under her chin, the stimulating flow of a shower, the taste of chocolate, the oboe reed at her lips and her fingers readying to press the keys.

At times I have to sit for what seems a ridiculously long time to remember how to start the car, how to turn on the TV or stereo, eat dinner, answer the phone, keep the calendar, pay attention to what someone is saying. I remember a similar disorientation and detachment when I first came under fire in combat and had to self-consciously make my infantryman's training instinctive. Much that was unconscious in the life I lived before now has to be found and made conscious with an effort that seems Herculean. We pass each other in the house as if we are sleepwalking, not speaking as we all search for the way to live our lives around the edge of the crater left by Lee's death.

My heart aches for Minnie Mae, a tough lady, a stoic whose suddenly aged face reveals her silent pain. No tears, just an enclosed sadness that has to be accepted as she moves on. We hold each other, of course, but not as much as I would have expected. Maybe if we hold each other too long, we won't be able to let go—and we have to go it alone, with the support of each other.

Minnie Mae seeks the kitchen and caretaking routines she has practiced so long, as her life became sublimated to her family. I feel guilty about the sacrifices made by this brilliant and talented woman, who was both a mezzo-soprano with distinguished local appearances and a commanding personal secretary who worked at the highest levels of the Pentagon during our war, but she has always said it was her choice and a happy one. I have never once heard her make a bitter remark about the difficult times in her life, and now I hope she will find some comfort in the routines of her kitchen, garden, laundry room; her office, where she keeps our accounts and pays our bills; my office, where she edits and types and reedits and retypes my revised pages in these last days of the age before computers.

Hannah, who will be a freshman in college next month, seems to be gathered into her large community of friends. I am most worried about Anne, who withdrew into herself more and more during the long hours in the waiting room and the survival days of burial and mourning that followed. She graduated from college as an art major and traveled in Europe on her own but has not yet found a career or even a job. She returned to waitressing at Newick's seafood restaurant, the only routine she had to hold on to at the time. It was Lee, the concerned middle child, who persuaded Anne to leave Newick's and share an apartment with her in Boston while Lee went to the conservatory. We spent the early summer finding that apartment, and now Anne, alone and without friends in Cambridge, will move into the empty apartment and begin an uncharted life.

But even the most normal habits by which we live most of our life aren't easy to perform. I can't remember a time when I couldn't read. Books have been my delight and escape all my life, from *The Little Engine That Could* to *Treasure Island* and *Robin Hood*. I wore out library cards, and when I received Kenneth Roberts's *Northwest Passage* from Uncle Will for my twelfth birthday, I read the night through by flashlight under the covers, finishing it as the sun came up. Even in combat I usually had a book with me that I would borrow from one Armed Forces library and return to the next one I found.

Now when I try to read, the pages blur, type running together into a tangled swamp of black ink, a vast delta I cannot map. I force myself to read slowly, to read out loud, terrified that I will lose this familiar form of escape when I most need it. Eventually I find I can read but I can't concentrate.

I make my way back to reading through the strongly plotted mystery novels that lack a complex plot but have a driving narrative force: Georges Simenon, Ed McBain. I especially escape into police procedurals, and I keep one or more by my bed so that when I slip from dreams of Lee to waking thoughts of Lee, all the what-ifs and if-onlys, I can flee to a book, reading a paragraph, the top one of the left-hand page where I always stop, as Lee did, then reading over a page and another page and yet another. As a writer and teacher of English, I am gaining a new respect for narrative and escape fiction. No more apologies for reading the nonacademic strong story, no hiding my secret addiction to mysteries and thrillers.

We sleep with the radio tuned to a classical music station, hoping that they will not play an oboe concerto. We keep a light on, and in the night Minnie Mae and I touch. She says nothing as I patrol the hall. When I return to our bedroom, a house length away, I pause to make sure the covers over Minnie Mae rise and fall.

16. Work

Soon after we bury Lee and before the fall begins, Dave Ellis, provost of the University of New Hampshire and a friend, calls me in my office, and we meet on the steps of Hamilton Smith Hall. We sit on the granite steps while he expresses the appropriate sympathy and concern. Then he makes a generous offer. I can take the next semester off with pay. I would be free of teaching and responsibility as English Department chairperson, and relieved of committee assignments. It is all I have ever wanted—time to write, time to read, time to remember. But not now. I am touched and terrified, knowing instantly that I need work. Duty, obligation, responsibility will be my therapy. Next month, in September, I will

return to my office at the university and to the classroom. By work, ritual, habit I will survive.

Dave understands but invites me to come see him if it
doesn't go well or if I need any relief or support. I thank
him, moved by the generosity of the university's offer—
and terrified at the thought of having time to remember,
to relive Lee's dying, to experience over and over again
our life.

It was work that saved me as a boy. Home was a
battleground, with the most effective weapon: silence.
We were masters of turning away. I realize now how
hard I tried to be a good son and a Christian soldier,
and how hopeless it was to try to behave in a way that I
thought would deliver love, or at least affection, at least
acceptance.

My not measuring up at home was a private failure,
but in school my humiliation was public. I recognize now
that I was bright, a compulsive reader far beyond my
grade level, a child artist, a scholar in my own way of top-
ics that interested me. I was, however, a sickly child who
was tutored through second grade and often kept at
home for long periods of convalesence most years. I was
nearsighted but until Uncle Will discovered it by acci-

dent when I was in the sixth grade, I believed that my inability to read the blackboard documented my stupidity. I was an only child and related better to adults than my classmates. And I was a fierce Baptist in a neighborhood of Irish Catholics, forced to play with boys and girls from an alien world my parents resented and feared. The rules of my home were filled with ironies I could not understand and advice that didn't work on the street. Although I was beaten at home, I was instructed to turn the other cheek in the playground. When I was beaten up by a bigger child, I was told that it was because my belief in Jesus Christ was too weak. Pray, I was told, and if I truly believed in Jesus, the bully's fist would be stayed. It was not.

Work, not religion, was my salvation. A morning and afternoon and Sunday paper route; shoveling snow; performing hated yard work; serving as a shabbas goy the one year we lived in an Orthodox Jewish neighborhood; organizing a real estate office; restoring antiques, cutting wood, and building a chapel during the four summers I was a "scholarship boy" at summer camp; making Scots sausage at Miller's Market, where I also kept track of the canned goods inventory, decorated the store windows, and stacked and sold fruit and vegetables, delivering with the store's truck before I had a truck license; serving as chauffeur for the state treasurer while I was in high school; cooking; house painting; unloading the inventory for the first supermarket in my neighborhood; quitting school in the spring of my tenth, eleventh, and twelfth grades to work on the *Boston Record and American*—all showed that getting to work early, running when others walked, and staying late could not earn me love but did produce respect—and money.

I worked my way through freshman year at Tilton Junior College by playing football and taking charge of a dormitory floor. In three years in the army I learned many unexpected skills, including how to leave a perfectly good plane in flight, and after the war, I supplemented the G.I. Bill by driving a Durham Laundry truck. I had one pride: I could do a day's work.

My work habits had gotten me jobs on newspapers and magazines, and when I was fired by *Time* magazine, it was my work habits that made it possible to survive for nine years as a freelance writer until I joined the faculty at the University of New Hampshire. Work was my way of life. It was my escape and my satisfaction. A job organized my day and concentrated my mind. Now work will allow me to survive the death of Lee.

But it isn't easy. Before I go to Ham Smith 103 to teach my first class I take a student I respect and trust aside, explain what happened (although they all knew), and ask the student to interrupt me if I wander off in a confusing monologue, to break a too-long silence, to snap me out of whatever other behavior is inappropriate, and to meet with me after class to tell me how it went.

I don't realize when I make the request how necessary it will be. When the students stand up to leave I am surprised but go to my office next door. This is a two-hour class in which there is little lecture but some instruction, some writing, and a great deal of question-and-answer discussion, but I have no memory of the class. Not one. I fear I have made a fool of myself, but the student reports I was the same as ever. This makes me laugh.

In each class I have a student watching out for me, but the classes, week by week, go along just fine, according to each "watcher," and we begin to laugh at how I am the same on autopilot as I was when I was consciously alert to every nuance of what was said and not said, each skeptical, challenging, or confused expression on a student's face.

I am also chair of an English department that has a full-time faculty of thirty or so and a part-time and graduate-student faculty of sixty. Numbly—and, I suspect, dumbly—I carry on and serve as well on the string of department, college, and university committees typical of the horizontal organization of an academic institution. This work—about which I have always continually complained, as does everyone else—becomes a salvation, a way to get through the hour. What do I do now? Ah, the tenure committee or the curriculum committee or the God-knows-what committee is meeting this afternoon. Do I belong to it? Yes. I go, I listen, and apparently I contribute, but I am not there.

I am not thinking all the time of Lee, but existing in a state of emotional paralysis. More than once I catch my face in the mirror and remember how those with whom I served in the army looked after returning from an action at the front. Stunned, drained of emotion, exhausted.

And I write. At least I open my notebook and pick up a pen, knowing that storytelling was my escape and salvation before I could write. I am a writer. That is what I do. It will now be my therapy.

My motto comes from Horace, *Nulla dies sine linea*— never a day without a line. I count words, as did Faulkner, Hemingway, Greene, and many other writers, and keep account of my productivity on yearly charts. On the thirty-first of July I wrote 1,801 words. In August, the column runs blank until the twenty-second, when I wrote 27 words. The next day I wrote 34, and that is all for the month. I thought I started writing earlier and that I clung to my daily writing as a sailor holds on to a life raft, but that is not true.

I remember trying to write every day beginning a few days after we buried Lee. I opened my daybook or journal, I uncapped my pen, I put paper in the typewriter, and I sat. Sitting, waiting, is the artist's discipline. Patience is essential, emptiness necessary. Wait and the page will fill. It always did, but after Lee's death it does not.

No words until September 3, when I write 66. Then 1,001 on the fourteenth, 189 the next day, then none, then 26, then three days before 288, two empty days, then 368, another empty day, then 30, two days without words, then 197 and two more days at the end of the month without a single word.

My daybooks are not diaries but a sort of common-place book, where I record the wisdom of writers and artists, make plans and outlines, exhort myself to be more regular in my habits, and record fragments of language that may grow into poems, articles, books. I look at what I wrote when I was teaching in the summer program in Vermont and accumulating pages of a novel. I am not the same person now. The pages were written by a stranger.

The next entry is 10/4/77, almost two months after Lee's death. The note is short: "Typed 502." I am writing again. There are a few notes about the novel, which I have not yet abandoned, and some manuscript pages on 10/10/77, 10/11/77, 10/12/77, a jump to 10/16/77, and then on 10/22/77 the first reference to Lee.

1957–1977

A column of air
ice hard
waits for an oboe
a woman
a song

I gasp. As I turn the page and read it with tears in my eyes, I think that Lee would have liked those lines I have so long forgotten. I draft a longer poem that does not work. And the next day I make several pages of notes on my continuing study of the writing process, which is the basis of my textbooks, and turn the page. I confront the raw wounds of loss:

COMFORT ME WITH ALTERNATIVES

She is not spider fat
with cancer
thin arms thin legs
pale smile

She does not stumble
into the room
twist at the ceiling
grunt out a word
need us to wipe her chin
after mocha chip ice cream

On such cold stones
I warm my hands

Five days later I ruin the poem or whatever it is with revision.

On 11/8/77, after a series of detached, professional academic notes, I suddenly write:

Lee, my laughing daughter lies dead.

Lee, who always stood in the crib in her yellow bedroom, laughing the day away. Lee who grumped out of the dentist's office, slumped in the chair and laughed at herself, will laugh no more.

Three quick, sharp lines, and then I do what I remember doing so often: change the subject abruptly, force my mind somewhere else:

Essay in celebration of rain

I am another person. I can't write about Lee. It is too early. Instead I write articles and talk about the writing process and the teaching of writing, gradually regaining my escape into language.

I am a soldier on a long march moving back toward the world in which I used to live but which will now never be the same. Slowly, out of habit, I hold on and make it from hour to hour, then day to day. No more, but it is enough. One more day without words. And then a day with words and another. In November, 7,417—about a third of my usual number. And then in December, the month of holiday and remembering, I write only five days for a total of 183.

And then in January 1978 I write every day; in fact I write every single day in 1978. I have gotten a firm hold on my life raft and am not about to let go.

17. Rage

It is one of those Indian summer days in October 1977 when the sun is July bright, the temperature just under hot, and the trees in New Hampshire filled with autumn scarlet, yellow, orange. At this time of year there is a softness to the air, a gentleness before winter storms. I am quietly driving along Islington Street in Portsmouth, car windows down, my elbow out in the breeze as it was when I was in high school and bought my first flivver. I realize that the tension in my arms, shoulders, legs, stomach is easing. I have begun to move toward acceptance, if not peace. Life will go on. We will all make it. I even feel an unexpected pride. We have been tested again and we have passed.

Driving has always been a stimulus to thinking for me. When I am stuck in writing, I go for a drive, not a walk. Behind the wheel is where I write in my head more than anywhere else. The habitual, routine tasks of driving and the ever-changing scenery seem to free my mind. This afternoon I reflect on the tests of my childhood–learning to ride a two-wheeler, learning to swim, learning to detach myself during the beatings at home. I relive the tests of the street ("Wanna knuckle sandwich?") and the tests of war (making my first parachute jump and surviving my first moments under enemy fire). The tests never seem to stop: marriage, divorce, remarriage, physical surgery, corporate surgery, the deaths of parents and close friends, and so many other tests we lose count of. But each of us has developed our own way of coping, and now we have passed the most demanding test of all. Lee would be proud of us. It is all right, I tell myself, to feel a bit smug. We have earned it.

Then I see a young woman wearing glasses standing on the curb. For a moment I think it is Lee, but it is not. Her hair is different, she holds herself in a way Lee would not, but ... As I slow and she steps into the crosswalk, a souped-up old hulk without a muffler swerves around me on the left, where there is no room to pass, and comes so close to the young woman that her skirt flares out in the car's wake and she staggers backward to the curb.

I take off after the car as if it had hit her and run. My rage is immediate and out of control. I get close enough to see his red hair, close enough to receive his one-fingered Roman salute. He drives faster and I drive faster. He could have killed her. He could have killed Lee. I am drunk with rage. The adrenaline pours in, and it feels good to be filled with virtuous anger. He suddenly turns down a street to the left, and I screech after him. All the driving skills I learned when I was a teenager be-hind the wheel, sharpened by the driving I did in the army as a military policeman and later as a police re-porter in Boston, are concentrated on catching him.

He turns right down an alley. So do I. He takes a right and accelerates on the straightaway. I keep up with him. He reverses direction and heads toward Market Square, where there surely will be police. To hell with that. I'll get him before them, pull him over to the curb, haul him out of the car the way I once did that driver on Route 1 in Ogunquit, bend him back over the hood, and with the hands that were trained as weapons in the paratroops, I will . . .

My car starts to slow. I remember how excited Lee, Anne, Hannah, even Minnie Mae got at how I dealt with that New York driver in his Caddy who tried to run us off the road, and I remember how ashamed, sad, and scared I had been when his neck was exposed to my hand. Slowly I get control of myself and pull over to the curb. I make myself take deep, calming breaths. I am surprised that it has taken so long for my rage to surface.

Rage is the child of impotence and guilt, and I felt both of those at the hospital and afterward. I am the father, the protector of my wife and children. It is as simple and elemental as that. That is my job. It may sound old-fashioned and sexist, even childish, but my feelings are my feelings, my inadequacy real, my guilt true. I failed Lee.

Right after her death I waited for the rage, but where could I aim my anger? There was no murderer on which to focus it, no rapist, no drunk driver, no hit-and-run, no mugging. She was attacked by an invisible virus. I could not rail at a God in which I do not believe. I could not be angry at the doctors who could not save Lee—I was at the hospital, I saw all they did, and I saw their own suffering at not being able to save her.

But the rage was there, and how good it felt for those stupid, dangerous moments during the chase. Now I feel silly about it, ashamed at my lack of control, appalled at how dangerously I drove, and yet I felt so good carried high on the river of rage—the best I have felt since that phone call to Vermont.

The guilt comes, but I put it to rest—most of it. Of course we feel guilty about being away in Vermont when Lee became fatally ill. But we were in Vermont so I could earn the money for her tuition at the New England Conservatory of Music.

We might not have supported her dream of becoming a musician. I even remember when an older sister of one of her friends dropped by to suggest that Lee major in accounting or something practical, but it was easy for a mother who had been a singer and father who was a writer to support, even celebrate, a dream of a life making music. We had just ordered the oboe she needed for the conservatory from France, and it had arrived in time for her to play it.

When she first brought Paul Lambert home I liked him, but his mother was Irish Catholic—the priority prejudice of my family and my childhood—and his father was French Canadian, the most popular prejudice of the state in which we lived, and he had even been to seminary. Could I find a scrap of prejudice left? Not one. Paul was a bright, humorous, caring young man. He enriched us all when we were with him, and Lee knew how we felt.

I worked to achieve a good relationship with my father long before he died. It was a relationship that functioned best at a distance and for short periods of time. The telephone was better than a visit. And the conversations were best when they focused on the unimportant, such as the Red Sox, and stayed clear of religion, politics, the family, and other important issues. But Mother? She never approved of me. Never could. She could never approve of herself, and so when she died, our relationship was full of what had not been said and now could never be said, what had been said and now could never be unsaid.

There was none of that with Lee. We were open with her and talked of what was important. I can't imagine the feelings of those who have an argument with a loved one and lose them to death before it is resolved. I know of a young person who said "I hate you" to a father who then dropped dead. It would be so easy for all of us, in a less dramatic way, to do the same thing. It does not even have to be a conflict unresolved but simply a failure to say "I love you."

Still, there is that subterranean feeling of guilt and certainly the impotence of not being able to protect her from this invisible enemy that invaded her body and slowly killed her. And should Lee have been given the gift of death? One week I am reading a magazine and come to an article that may have suggested a flat brain wave is not an accurate sign of death. I do not know if that is what the article really says, for I shut the magazine, toss it in the trash, and go to do some task on which I could concentrate.

And even inappropriate guilt and impotence lead to rage. Since I chased that driver in Portsmouth, I have often felt the same anger, but I have never again let that lion out of the cage.

I attend a party of celebration in the home of close friends, one of many I have been to over the years for birthdays, for anniversaries, grants received, promotions earned. All at this party are faculty colleagues and their partners. We have served on committees together, gossiped and grumped with them, attended concerts and taken trips to museums together, gone out to dinner with them or had them in for dinner. We know their children and they know ours. Most of those who gave us such extraordinarily sensitive caring when we lost Lee are here, and one of them, drink in hand but not drunk, is chatting genially with several of us when he says, "Well, at last she's gone. We've gotten rid of our daughter and have our house to ourselves again."

I feel the rage in my hands, in my arms, in the way I shift my weight on my feet. Those around us are laughing, nodding; in fact, I may be laughing myself. I have been socialized to act in a way I do not feel. He is a genial man, a good husband, father, teacher, colleague, but I want to yell, "Don't say that. Never say that, you son of a bitch. Your daughter is alive. Mine is gone. Yours may as well die too, and then you'll have your fucking empty house to yourself, all right. Her leaving is not to be celebrated." My hand wants to slug him, knock him down. I want to kick him, make him hurt the way I hurt, but of course I turn away, walk outside, stand alone until I am calm and can rejoin the party.

He and I will continue to be good friends, growing even closer in our mutual retirements. Sadly, I will live to comfort him when his daughter does die and later still when his wife is lost to Alzheimer's, and I will stand by his sons at his grave, but I often think of his innocent remark and my visceral rage.

At such parties, during meals with friends, and in sidewalk conversations in the months after Lee's death, I often feel the way I did when I first came home from combat after World War II—an alien in my homeland. My familiar life has been altered by this loss, and I feel as if I am seeing my world through binoculars turned the wrong way.

I become irrationally sad at the angry faces I see on teenagers and their parents at the supermarket or on the sidewalk. Don't let these precious years be lost, I want to tell them, but, of course, I don't. What seemed significant in the murky world of academic guerrilla warfare now seems trivial, and all that seems trivial has dropped off the screen. I want to call a department meeting and say,

"Let's trust each other, respect each other, love each other. We came to teaching English because of a love of reading, language, and writing. Let's celebrate, not fear our diversity. We are all doing good work. Life is fragile; enjoy it when you can."

I don't do that, but I find that some members of my department have not signed up for the health plan that is free and that others have not contributed to the retirement plan, where their contributions will be matched by the university. My suggestions are not appreciated—or acted upon. I learn that many acquaintances, apparently unable to face their mortality, have no financial wills and no living (really dying) wills, and I try to persuade them to take action now. None does.

I have to accept my alienation and hope that eventually I will not live at such a distance, but I cannot always suppress my rage.

I drive alone to an academic meeting in another part of the state through the early autumn landscape of southern New Hampshire. Ever since I first had my own wheels, (neither my father or mother owned or ever drove a car), I have liked driving alone, the road unreeling before me, my hands feeling each curve, my foot light on the accelerator, allowing the momentum and the falling of the hills to do as much as they can. Riding the brake or the gas pedal seems proof of a poor driver.

I usually make the driving more of a challenge than it is, trying to lay a proper line over the hills and around each curve, but today I cannot play the game of driving that has always brought me relief. And I, who have always sought aloneness—the city messenger boy, the army soldier on lonely patrol, the reporter working alone to get the story—now wish I had passengers, to whose babble I would have to pay attention.

The driving, as it often does, releases my mind to the rumination from which effective teaching and writing come. The mechanical act seems to stimulate the collision of unexpected ideas, the arrival of scenes and images that make the familiar strange or the unexpected familiar, the connection and disconnection of fragments of language from which writing grows, the double and triple exposures of memories with present or future that increases the texture of living. But today my mind will not let go of Lee.

I sit again with her, as I did only weeks ago in the orchestra she was rehearsing with. I see her looking back at me over her shoulder in delighted terror years before as I push the swing higher and higher. I take her hand again as we walk to first grade. I hold her in my arms late at night, making comforting circles on her tiny back until her crying becomes sobbing, then her sobbing, sleep. I turn on the car radio, but the memories will not stop. I hear her practice a phrase from Albioni from the other room again and again, see her looking at Paul with love and delight. I drive faster, taking the hill curves at a speed that demands total concentration, but still I cannot stop the flood of memory. I remember long, grown-up conversations when she was concerned with her mother, sisters, my work, or her own future, talks that I thought foreshadowed the decades of such wise helpful conversations we would share in the many years ahead. I suddenly swerve the car to the edge of the road and bring it to a bouncing stop in some weeds across the fence from a startled cow, yank open the door, and howl. The cow takes off, and I hear sounds rising from my throat that I have never heard before, sounds of loss and death and rage and despair that seem prehistoric, that come from before language. Howl after howl comes from me until at last they stop and I weep.

18. Emptiness

Twenty-four years have rushed past when I walk down the corridor to the room with the name Lee still on the door to wake Karl, a brother-in-law she never knew. When Anne, her older sister, visits with her husband and their daughter, Michaela Lee, I get up in the dark of Sunday, wake Karl, and we go out sketching the way other fathers and sons go hunting or fishing. We meet Bill Childs, who was Anne's—and Lee's—art teacher in high school, on the riverbank that offers a view of Exeter, New Hampshire, the gently winding river and the factories-turned-condominiums on the other side.

Bill and Karl work in oils, and I sketch in ink and crayon. The rising sun reveals a mackerel sky that the wind soon washes clean, and the river turns each scene upside down, reflecting shape and color. It is ideal for drawing and painting, but each of us is dissatisfied in his own way. I am less concerned than my companions, who are artists. They have more on the line, even Karl, who is forced to be a part-time artist although he has full-time energy, discipline, and drive. I have learned that when the writing goes badly or doesn't go at all, I am often on the insecure brink of a breakthrough. The line on the page or in my mind will show me something— a fragment, a shape, a color, a tension between images— and lead me somewhere I did not expect to go. That is what we who write, draw, or compose have to accept: our ignorance, our instructive failures, our blessed clumsiness or awkwardness that shows us what we can't yet do but must.

I am fortunate to receive instruction from the diuretic that was just prescribed for fluid in my seventy-six-year-old lungs. I have—right now—to desert art for a men's room. On the way I realized that I want—no, need— to draw the emptiness, the nothingness, the space that has been left in our lives by Lee's departure.

When I return to the riverbank, I take my sketchbook

and draw two jagged, torn-edged lines a couple of inches apart and then sketch the ends of our house with the ragged space torn across our lives. The drawing is not good, but that doesn't matter. It is the process, not the product, that counts. I know I will be drawing the spaces where she is not for some time. When I show it to Bill, he says, "The nothing is a shape itself. That adds contradiction, ambivalence." And as artists, we know those elements are good. There is always a stimulating lack of conclusion in an effective painting or piece of writing, a significant lack of completeness that lets the viewer or reader in. The work belongs to the individual viewer or reader, not to the maker. In the drawing as in life, Lee is here and not here, an emptiness and a force.

In the years since Lee's departure I have published a few poems and columns about her, but until the writing of this book I have not allowed myself to spend hours in those cold rooms of memory.

One of the personal and artistic problems is how to deal with emptiness, that column of air waiting for her oboe. This morning I pass an empty field, rich with new spring grass, but see only its emptiness. Usually I take

pleasure in the tidal flow of fields that seem to move under wind or shadow, or I see them with an infantry soldier's eyes as a space to cross under fire with the rise and
fall of the field hardly visible but giving the soldiers
places to drop and take cover. And then there are days
like today, when the empty fields remind me of the space
in my life left empty by Lee's leaving.

I try not to speculate about Lee's life as a musician,
her husband or children, or where she would live. I don't
try to populate that tall column of emptiness that runs
through my life. I miss the casual conversations we have
not had, the communication of gesture, glance, or movement, the anticipation of a visit or its memory.

It is still achingly hard never to hear her voice from
the other room, never to pick up the phone and talk
to her. I even miss the worries that I would have had
for her, the anxieties about her health, her safety, her career, her family or lack of family, the decisions that might
be wrong, her happiness. I have not told her my worries
about her mother; she has not known of my bypass, the
short-term but dark depressions of my later years. She
has not read one of my more than seven hundred *Boston*

Globe columns or the eleven books and fourteen revised editions I have published since her death. She doesn't even know I have retired from teaching.

We have not sent her cards from Norway, Denmark, Tuscany, or all the other places we have traveled without her. There are hundreds of classical compact discs I have not bought for her, books we have not shared, meals we have not eaten together, jokes we have not laughed at. She does not know my beard has grown white, that Minnie Mae has Parkinson's. Can it be that she has never seen my computers, never owned one of her own?

This column of emptiness that runs through my life always surprises me. She must have known Hannah's Michael—a musician, as she was. They must have had conversations about music, listened to concerts or CDs and heard what I could not hear. She must have known Karl and his painting, his cooking. It seems impossible that she has not held Joshua, Sam, or Michaela as infants, that they have never run across the room to Aunt Lee.

Sometimes I mention Lee and catch myself. So many of my closest friends never knew her, people like Chip and Lisa and Kell and Brock and Tom, who seem to have been my friends forever, although they are younger than

I am. It cannot be that they did not know Lee, or that she did not know them. But it is. She is not even a memory or an emptiness in their lives.

Lee would be sad that her mother has never sung since her child died. That spring she gave her last performance. The songs Minnie Mae performed with such passion, sadness, and power were a terrible foreshadowing. She sang Gustav Mahler's Kindertotenleider, songs on the death of children.

Lee would be unhappy that her absence makes us unhappy, that her not being is a space in her mother's life and her sisters', a space even in the lives of my sons-in-law and our grandchildren. I think of Aunt Helen, my mother's younger sister, who died in the flu epidemic of 1919, five years before I was born, and whose not being was such a part of my life. Even as a child, I was aware I did not know her and never would. I tried to imagine her as a happier woman than Mother, prettier, more caring. She was a nurse and she died caring for others.

The air in that column of nothingness is not cold. It is nothing. It is—most of the time—a gentle absence, something missing that at its best gives meaning to all the small importances I might have overlooked, makes me listen to those who are here, be aware of what a loss it would be if they were not. Her not being makes the being of all the others in my life brighter, stronger, more significant, and for that Lee would be grateful, as am I.

Time, however, does not close the edges of the emptiness. Instead it grows larger. First there is not the middle child who was in the center of the family picture; then, when there is one wedding picture, then another, the gap grows larger. She does not add a husband to those who step into the family portrait and, later, none of the children that she might have had; in our private, unspoken vision, there will be no children of her children.

Finally in age, our children become our parents, concerned for us, giving us parental guidance and certain love. The emptiness grows larger. In losing a child out of the natural order, we have lost the child who would become a parent at the farther end of life.

19. Sightings

It is six in the morning, and Bob Karelitz slides into the booth at Young's to talk hockey. Bob is a dentist in Dover, a fellow hockey fan, and a neighbor. His wife is a writer of books who plows the same field I do. I knew her before I knew him. I've met his folks many times, seen his children grow older, seen Bob's hair recede and grow gray, noticed his face develop the interesting lines that life draws on us all. Suddenly the talk turns to Julius Erving when the famous basketball player was at the University of Massachusetts. Bob saw him on the basketball floor and in the dorm, and I realize this middle-aged jock friend may have been at UMass at the same time as Lee. I check up. They overlapped by a year.

The booth dips and twirls with my sudden vertigo, the beginning of another headache. Lee is forever twenty. I have not seen her age and develop the more interesting face that age grows on us. And I will never see her age. I explain my sudden mood change to Bob, and the world rights itself.

But all day my head keeps trying to draw a forty-four-year-old face on Lee. She should not remain forever young, but she does—and she is always just around the corner, driving the car that passes and is gone, leaving the sidewalk and entering the store just ahead. But when I pass the store window she is never there.

I remember one of those rare moments when all my worlds seemed in balance. We were on a tour of Tuscany, but that day we had skipped the round of cathedrals. Minnie Mae chose to read and rest in the hotel, and I took my sketchbook and wandered through the narrow, bustling streets of Siena, to my mind a far more beautiful city than Florence.

Although I live in New Hampshire and have spent time in the woods, I am a city boy, and the ultimate city experience for me is in Italy. As a young man, I spent hours sauntering alone or with young ladies along the lived-on streets of Boston's North End with people who wore their feelings outdoors, so unlike my Scots family. They gestured with hands and body, sometimes twirling, bowing, jumping to make a point. They made faces, they stood near each other, they yelled, whistled, touched, they ate on the sidewalk, they minded everyone else's business, and they laughed—oh, how they laughed.

At the end of my war I was in Italy on special duty, still in my paratrooper combat jumpsuit, an American flag sewn on my sleeve. I was the enemy, yet everywhere I went I was treated to smiles. Some of these men and women must have had their husbands, children, fathers killed or wounded by troops dressed in my clothes, but they all welcomed me, even when I went alone into the areas that were off-limits. Once, as I stood watching a fair in a park in Milan, my sleeves rolled up, my arm reaching out to a tree, a young woman came up and kissed the inside of my elbow, softly, slowly.

Ah, romance.

Ah, commerce. She named a price and took no offense when I smiled and shook my head.

I thought of that kiss a generation later as I walked the streets of Siena. I had memories but no destination, no plan, no agenda as I turned down one twisty alley, climbed stone stairs at the end, entered a tunnel of a street, then suddenly took a step out into a square that exploded with sunlight. The entire square was paved, and it sloped down into a sort of a stone pond. It was filled with people—not too many tourists on that warm September afternoon, mostly Italians enjoying their world.

I sat at a table and ordered a beer. I opened my sketchbook and started to draw the buildings that edged the square. Under my pen they became alive, a row of structures that were elbowing each other, tipping, leaning, somehow growing into each other, an architectural animal lolling in the sun, gently breathing.

People came by and watched me sketch. Usually I am too shy for that. I am no artist. I just draw to see, discover, remember. But I didn't mind their curiosity that afternoon. Of course they were interested in me, they were interested in everybody. I have rarely felt so at peace as I did that afternoon as I sketched and watched the curved shadows grow long across the grand oblong square.

Suddenly it was time to pack up and go back to the hotel to get Minnie Mae and head out to dinner, but as I left the square, Lee—a young woman now, assured and happy, swinging her arms, freed of her backpack—turned the corner not fifteen yards away and was gone.

I strode after her, hearing my voice shout, "Lee!" It was Italy. No one paid attention. Everyone shouted. I saw Lee ahead, just a bit farther away, and walked faster.

What was she doing here? Had she survived in life as she had in my dream? Was this where she went when she left intensive care? I was gaining on her. I started jogging, following the kerchief she had tied over her head. She would be thirty now—no, thirty-five—but I wouldn't be angry at her for not getting in touch with us. She was here and alive.

I started to run, and she turned a corner and was gone. The street was empty, the first empty street I can ever remember having seen in Italy. A street of silence and closed shutters and dark shadow, and Lee was gone. Again.

It doesn't happen often, but it happens too often. Never on an anniversary, a birthday, a holiday. It is always unexpected—sometimes caught out of the corner of an eye, sometimes straight on. This morning during breakfast at Young's she is facing me in the last booth on the left. She is with a boy, like when she was a freshman in college. I have aged, but she has not. It is not Lee, I tell myself. It can't be, but it is—until she stands up and is short, heavy-thighed, not Lee at all. Not even close, and I feel sadness, not relief. I will never see Lee again.

Writing this book has not been as hard as people expect. They think I have put the loss of Lee behind me, but I have not. Lee is with me every day. Not as frequently as the living, but there, just at the edge of the door, in the other room, nearby but out of sight—most of the time.

In the afternoon I am examined by a new cardiologist, and I am pleased with him and his approach to cardiac care. My heart is still beating, but he cannot really tell if the pump needs more repair until he receives records of the bypass fourteen years ago, the angioplasty six years ago, and the results of tests that may reveal the need for still more tests. The clock is ticking.

I welcome the echocardiogram, followed by a two-day Cardolite stress test—I have a greater fear of the imagined unknown than the experienced known—but Minnie Mae, who sat in on the examination, and I need a change of mood that evening. We watch Nathan Lane's astonishing tribute to Danny Kaye with the Boston Pops. I see the grin on Minnie Mae's face and feel the same relaxed smile on my own.

Then when Lane leaves the stage, the orchestra plays several Russian compositions, closing with Ravel's transcription of Mussorgsky's *Pictures at an Exhibition*. I've just played that on my car stereo, and I am delighted to see the instruments I have been hearing being played, especially the great clashing Zilgian cymbals. Suddenly, during a quiet passage, I see a woman in the oboe section, just at the edge of the screen. It is Lee.

Of course it is not Lee. She doesn't look like Lee, is thinner, has blond hair, but how do I know what Lee would look like at forty-four? It could be Lee. It could have been Lee. She had been accepted to the New England Conservatory of Music to study under a member of the Boston Symphony Orchestra.

Several Christmases ago I saw Lee in a Swedish choir, not playing oboe but singing like her mother. The camera kept returning to her face. It was Lee. She had recovered and escaped the hospital mortuary, had gone to Europe, married a Swede, spoke Swedish, sang in a Swedish choir.

I still feel the certainty from a decade or more ago when I saw her playing oboe with the Vienna Philharmonic. She has performed in Berlin and New York and San Francisco. I have been good at not investing my ego in my living daughters' careers, but Lee? I still have dreams for Lee.

We sold her new French oboe, for which she waited so long, refusing to let us spend money for such a good instrument unless she was sure. Well, she had become sure, and had played her new oboe a few times, and had dreams of trying the cello, perhaps composing, perhaps conducting. Perhaps.

I collect records, and when Lee became interested in the oboe, I bought many more recordings of oboe performances. It was a way of supporting her ambitions, and it was music we could share. Now I realize they were all on LPs. Lee never heard a CD, never even heard of a CD player. She was ten years dead when I bought my first CD.

After she died, I could not play the oboe recordings. I still can't, but I no longer rush to turn off the FM when an oboe solo comes on, not always, not even if it is one she rehearsed again and again, the notes flowing stronger and more easily with each practice session. The notes stay in our house, coming from the room where she practiced twenty-four years before. I wonder if, after we are gone and the house is sold, the new owners will hear some leftover notes from time to time. I hope so.

A few years ago Minnie Mae and I were eating lunch in a Japanese noodle restaurant next door to Symphony Hall in Boston when a gaggle of musicians, some about twenty years old, came in talking about their last performances and the next. I am one who often talks with the people at the next table. I start to ask if they know Lee.

But they were not yet born when Lee died. They are young, with their living—if they are lucky—ahead of them. Lee would be in her forties, an established professional, a mother at home with her children, a music teacher. Perhaps she would be something else: a writer, a psychologist, a businesswoman. How can we predict an unlived life? There is no escape from what might have been.

The phone rings, and I grab it quickly, as is my habit, made immediate each time because of that phone call to Vermont so few, so many years ago.

"I'd like to speak to Lee Murray."

It is always a surprise, always unexpected. I am never

prepared. Usually I just hang up, but tonight I hear my voice, tight, tense, carefully controlled, say, "So would I. She died twenty-four years ago."

I hate the cold reality of my words and feel the anger rising. I tell myself it is not the telemarketer's fault. She may have lost her own child.

"Is Lee Murray home?"

The voice didn't hear what I said. I let my voice rise, make myself speak slowly. Minnie Mae hears my tone and turns to look at me.

"Lee Murray is not at home. My daughter died twenty-four years ago."

"She has won a chance for a trip to the Bahamas."

I am yelling, "My daughter is dead! Didn't you hear? My daughter is dead."

The slight burning across my chest will increase if I do not make myself calm. I gently put the phone back in its cradle.

Minnie Mae and I are together without words. It happens. Lee is called by a radio station or has a chance to have her rugs cleaned or to take a beauty course or have her siding replaced. The mail brings credit card offers, an invitation to become a student at a business school, a chance to contribute to a college from which she never graduated. A dentist who never looked in her mouth sends her a reminder for a cleaning or a card for the birthday she will never celebrate.

Each time it happens, we sit without speaking, allowing the memories to flow through us like a river rising toward flood tide, then will them to slowly retreat. After the Pops concert is over, we are not yet ready for bed, for the possibility of the night thoughts that make sleep retreat. We concentrate on the Red Sox game on television, follow the low-and-away pitch Pedro Martinez of the Red Sox uses to strike out another left-handed batter. Thank God for the triviality of sports. We watch the slow ballet of baseball until the flood of memories recedes and we dare to attempt sleep.

20. Fear

I pull into the garage and haul myself out of the car, and as soon as I unlock the door from the garage into the house I see the insistent blinking of the answering machine in the kitchen. We have been away all afternoon—lunch out, Staples, Wal-Mart, DeMoula's supermarket, Water Street Bookstore—and I forgot once again to turn on the cell phone I keep in the car against emergencies. I didn't carry it in with me to the stores, not while we ate a sandwich at Subway. I didn't check to see if there was a message at home.

I dump the groceries and run through the study, almost tripping on the step up to the kitchen, where I punch the blinking button. It is more than twenty-four years since we were away and didn't get the call to come home immediately because Lee was terribly sick.

It is a hang-up.

The anxiety isn't first. The guilt comes first. The unnamed guilt that has been suppressed by reason. Then the anxiety. Stumbling to the answering machine, I ran through my checklist: It isn't Minnie Mae, she's getting out of the car. Anne should be at work; the same for Hannah. Josh, Sam, Michaela at school. Karl and Michael at work.

I start to call Hannah. She may be home today, but I can't keep her schedule straight. Perhaps I should call Anne at work. Ridiculous, I tell myself, and go back to the car for the groceries and the books I bought at Water Street. Minnie Mae, in the slow motion of Parkinson's, is just making it around the car.

"Who was on the phone? Is everyone all right?"

"Just a hang-up," I say, as if she was silly to worry. We put the groceries away, and I can't resist picking up the phone and dialing Hannah. She is at home, and I ask, "Did you call? Is everything all right?"

She is not surprised. She knows as well as we do that twenty-four years ago is yesterday, that what can't happen here can. We live on a fragile membrane of life that bends under our weight and sometimes tears but has not broken again. But it will.

And yet, sitting with a glass of wine before supper, I try to feel silly at my neurotic imagination and can't. The ties to Minnie Mae, to my daughters and their children and their husbands, are what give meaning to my life. I am bound to them and they to me. We worry about one another. We fear what may happen and what most certainly will happen one day, in the natural order of things or, as we all know, in a random, unnatural order.

After Lee's death I am surprised by my friends who live in confidence, who have parents, even grandparents still alive. I too had an irrational innocence when Lee became sick, a confidence that she would survive, that it couldn't be happening to my family, that medical science would save her.

I should not have felt such confidence. I was born in sin, bred to fear in a Scots family that attempted to hide its dour nature with an occasional false jollity. We believed in hellfire and damnation, and I was warned of all the dangers of the world, such as getting blood poisoning from rusty nails, sitting on cold stone and not being able to have babies, drafts that brought the killer pneumonia, bruises that became cancer, drowning from swimming less that two hours after eating, drinking milk with lobster (they would not answer my questions about lobster bisque and stew), Irish Catholic girls who wanted to make babies, redheaded girls even if they were not RC, choking on fish bones.

In my childhood I had whooping cough, German measles and regular measles, bronchitis each winter, mumps, boils, double lobar pneumonia when I was in a coma for five days and saved by prayer. Each night I recited, "If I die before I wake, I pray the Lord my soul to take." Father took to bed when sales fell. Mother had an ulcer that didn't heal during all the years I knew her. Grandmother was bedridden from a "shock."

I served as a paratrooper in combat, where most of the soldiers I knew were killed or wounded. I controlled my paralyzing fear in battle by deciding I would die, and yet, close call after close call, I also believed I was a survivor.

But a great medical center could not save Lee, and ever afterward our normal fears for our children and each other increased. It could happen to us. We were the unfortunate family across town, the grieving parents on page one staring at the dark hole in the ice.

When we returned to the hospital six weeks or so after Lee's death to be given medical reports and the result of the autopsy, we were invited to ask questions. Anne, I think, asked the first: "Will we get Reye's syndrome?"

The answer was that it was not likely that Anne and Hannah were vulnerable. I was shocked not at her question but at the fact I had never thought of the question. At that moment I knew for sure that we would all live with fear. Not just of Reye's syndrome but of all the terrors of the world in a special way. What certainly could not be could. I thought of the children my daughter would have and how what had happened to Lee would be with them as parents. And, of course, I knew that as long as Minnie Mae and I live we will have a special concern for them.

I have come to believe that innocence is not a good thing. We must know the possible—that lump that may be cancer, the cough that is more than a cough, the pain that calls for attention. Perhaps if it were not for Lee I might not have paid attention to the funny feeling that was a heart attack and I asked my good friend Chip Scanlan to drive me to the hospital.

Minnie Mae and I are the ones to urge our friends to see a doctor, and it is with irony that we encourage our friends to go to the medical center sixty-plus miles away in Boston, since it was at MGH that my father died and eight years later where we lost Lee.

Each of us has had, in his or her own way, to learn to live with a responsible, intelligent fear. I wanted to go into combat with soldiers who had fear. I knew a few who did not, and they all were killed because of their stupid courage; often they took many of the rest of us with them. Having fear is necessary, and then it is essential to control that fear. Fear is our sixth sense, and we have to pay attention to its messages, then go on to live as best we can. And those of us who have lost a family member live the rest of our lives intimate with fear, always answering the phone, prepared to do what may have to be done.

As we gave the gift of death to Lee, it may be that one of her gifts to us is fear, the awareness of the fragility of life. The dragons in the shadows are real, and if they attack, we can survive to live a rich if fearful life.

21. Acceptance

Minnie Mae is at the stove and I am reaching for something in the refrigerator when the phone rings. I listen and turn to my wife. "It is breast cancer."

It is more than twenty years since we survived the loss of Lee, but the process of acceptance continues. We are experienced at bad news and share an unspoken confidence that we will survive. We go on getting supper, not talking about the uninvited guest that has joined us but not ignoring its presence either. We have learned not to withdraw into silence but to talk, to try on the word we have so feared—cancer—and to prepare ourselves for what lies ahead. By eight o'clock that evening the process of acceptance is complete. Our focus is on what to do next.

In the appointments that quickly follow—surgeon, oncologist, radiologist—I am not surprised by Minnie Mae's courage and practical, down-to-earth attitude, but I am astonished at the nature of her responses to the questions she has to answer.

She suffers from Parkinson's, a disease that means that she—and those around her—live life in slow motion. The patient is slow to get out of bed, slow to dress, slow to walk, slow to eat, slow to talk, slow to respond. Yet when Minnie Mae is asked to make the decision between mastectomy and lumpectomy, she listens to the advantages and disadvantages of each procedure and then speaks quickly. "Lumpectomy." The same was true of decisions about radiation and chemotherapy.

She has, unfortunately, had experience with acceptance. The death of a child is certainly a test and an exploration of acceptance.

Minnie Mae and I have brought balance to each other. I want to spend, she wants to save; I want to act now, she wants to act later; I see the glass half full, she sees the glass half empty.

When we took Lee to Massachusetts General Hospital, Minnie Mae prepared herself for the worst by accepting

Lee's death from the beginning. She was using a technique I often used: to prepare for the worst by accepting it prematurely. And with the anger against the fates that is always with us at such times, I felt that Minnie Mae was betraying Lee. The more I knew she was right, the madder it made me. I would be the one who had hope, even when there was no hope.

It could have been one of those great fault lines that destroy a marriage, but it was not primarily because of Minnie Mae's prenuptial wisdom, declaring that our relationship must be built as much, perhaps more, on respect as on passion.

It takes a long time to accept the death of a child. We made the decision to remove extraordinary means, called the funeral home, told family and friends, walked the Durham cemetery to pick out a lot, held the service, saw the grave filled over as if we were actors in a play.

We each had a role to play, a role given us by tradition, our culture, our ethnic background, our family history, our personalities: sisters, mother, father, close friends, all behaving the way that we have been instructed, more than we knew, in how to behave.

We did it well. But it was not us, not yet.

I remember the strange detachment I felt when people gave me sympathy. I needed it—oh, how I needed it, especially touching and holding, a caring beyond speech—and yet I was outside the person who was being comforted. I was watching a father being comforted. It could not be me. But I knew how to behave. To allow the tears to flow if they came, to resist the tears if I could, to accept the comfort in whatever form it took—a casserole, a letter, a handshake or hug, words clumsy with caring, a look. I thanked the givers in the way I should. And I was conscious of playing the role of male, being strong for Minnie Mae, Anne, Hannah.

I remember some of the same feelings I had in combat: an uncomfortable pride that I was able to play the role, a feeling that the role was dishonest. I was not strong, brave, composed; I should break under this weight. Since my war I often wondered if those who broke under fire were the sane, those of us who did not insane.

And yet I knew the role of strong, grieving father would save me, just as the role of brave soldier had saved me at war. And I did know that the role would eventually become the person. I would grow into it.

It was only ten years ago, when I suffered my heart attack, that I realized that acceptance is a kind of aggression. It isn't giving up. It isn't passive. It is concentrating all one's living on the moment and what has to be done to survive. During the heart attack I felt no fear, just an intense calm, a focus. I remember how, when I was a child, I learned to float after summers of terror. I had to give myself up to the water to survive. I had to learn to relax, to discover my buoyancy, to swim in water over my head and make it back to shore.

We had to accept the finality of Lee's death. It was simple. Clear. True. And so hard to make it part of what we were. There would be no recovery. I saw her death as similar to losing a leg. It was gone. The person who lost it would never wake and find it had grown back. The leg that was not there would hurt and we would have to accept this private and mysterious hurt, but we would go on as the amputee goes on, the missing leg becoming part of who that person is.

We would not recover from Lee's death. We were forever changed, and we would have to accept all it meant, including a strange, powerful, and discomforting pride. If we could accept her death and go on, we would be able to accept Minnie Mae's breast cancer, her Parkinson's, my heart attack, bypass, and angioplasty, our diabetes, my glaucoma, Minnie Mae's many eye operations.

Lee would understand the irony of our exchange of gifts. We gave her the gift of death, and she gave us the gift of acceptance.

22. Sharing

When we moved to New Jersey before Lee and Hannah were born, we were shocked at the price of Christmas trees, so we waited until Christmas Eve, when the prices fell, to buy our tree. This became a family custom, and when we moved to New Hampshire, we added the custom of cutting our own tree—on Christmas Eve.

The day before the first Christmas without Lee we knew the importance of custom, habit, ritual—all lifelines to grip when the seas become rough. Anne, Hannah, Minnie Mae, and myself went to a neighbor who sold cut-your-own Christmas trees.

Christmas is always an emotional time for me. Mother hated holidays, I think because she feared she would do something wrong and so, of course, she did. We had the only artificial tree anyone had seen in the 1930s. Many of my gifts were tossed angrily at me in the brown paper wrappings in which they arrived, and yet I was also spoiled by gifts my folks couldn't afford, as if Mother was trying to buy an affection she felt she could not earn. It was the pattern, I understand, of the alcoholic mother by a woman who was a life member of the Women's Temperance Union.

My childhood family gatherings seemed to me to be full of cruel humor—whoopee cushions, hinged spoons, water glasses with holes—and a false heartiness that could not cover the underground river of dislike and prejudice and guilt I could sense but not understand. As a result, in my own family I have made a great deal of Christmas, with many presents and ritual upon ritual: Minnie Mae's Christmas stollen, cookies, decorating the tree, stockings on doorknobs. But the happiness I experienced with my family was always shadowed by childhood holidays that I could flee but not quite escape.

And now Lee was gone. We tramped out in the knee-high snow and I fell behind, remembering the snows in the Battle of the Bulge and the dead resting under the cover of new-fallen snow. I hardly paid attention to what was going on until Anne and Hannah hollered that they had the tree. It was the scrawniest, most twisted tree on the lot, an ugly duckling of a tree, and one of my daughters explained that this year we should give a home to the ugliest Christmas tree we could find. We could love, celebrate, and decorate this tree, which no one else would ever choose. I weep as I write and rewrite this moment.

That act and the tree that stood sentinel to all our ceremonies set the tone for a Christmas that I will never forget. We had young people in whose parents were away. Somehow our loss made us reach out, not withdraw.

We were all changed by the loss of Lee, and it was not all bad. A few days after we came home from the hospital I was in the local grocery when I saw a faculty member I knew but did not like pushing his wife along in a wheelchair. She suffered from some dreadful brain disease. I had never met her, and normally I would have skedaddled down a different aisle, but this day I found myself going to her, taking her hand, chatting with her.

When Minnie Mae was going through her radiation for breast cancer, she needed me close by to help her with her bra, and so I sat by the patients' dressing area, where there was a constant flow of people going to radiation or chemotherapy, and for those six weeks I was part of a community that was remarkably open, direct, unembarrassed, and with a black sense of humor that reminded me of combat.

We became family for a neighbor widow who passed through a series of hospital and nursing home visits, and again I found that it had become normal for me to speak even to those who could not acknowledge me. I had learned from our staying away from Lee during her slow dying that you do not have to be a professional to speak, to smile, to touch.

I don't go around like some cheery Donald of Sunnybrook Farm, but ever since we lost Lee, I feel comfortable around people who might have made me uncomfortable in the past. Partly it is a tribute to Lee, who cared so much for everyone, but mostly it is the fact that I now belong to a larger community.

There were people who could not speak to me after Lee's death. Perhaps they didn't know what to say; perhaps they thought bad luck was contagious. The same thing happened after my heart attack and bypass. There were not many people like this, but enough to make me feel isolated, not recognized. I have learned the power of a smile, the importance of touch, and I know that avoidance is the worst human crime.

When most people discover that someone they meet has lost a child, they are usually silent. They don't know what to say but communicate in a few mumbled words, a reaching out, a look of understanding and compassion, and a silence that has a strange kind of bleak comradeship in it. One reason for me to write this book is to break that silence, to speak of what usually causes silence.

I have recently tried to do this with people I meet, asking about their loss and talking about mine. I find these conversations at first tentative, hesitant, then fluent. The person who isn't visible to others becomes visible. The conversation may take place in a supermarket line, during a hockey game, when you stop by a table at lunch, or during a short walk or a long drive.

There are organized therapy groups both with and without professional direction, and I respect the work they do and the comfort they bring, but Minnie Mae and I are not joiners. I have discovered we don't need to be.

All we have to do is to take the opportunity to speak. We will say the right thing. There is no wrong thing to say. Only silence is wrong. We know the territory. The conversation can last a minute or fifteen; it can be with a stranger who becomes a friend or a stranger you never see again.

Robert Frost said that a poem is "a momentary stay against confusion." That describes these moment of sharing. They are usually casual, often passing, usually with people you may not speak with again, but they are important moments that enrich our lives and give us the strength to go on, knowing we are not alone. We are survivors.

23. Celebration

I look up from my computer and watch sunlight settle on a single maple leaf. The leaf trembles, and I speculate on the weight of sunlight. Then a slight breeze saunters through the tree and I take account of the changing pattern of sunlight and shadow.

It isn't much.

And it is everything. If Lee had risen from her bed in intensive care, one of the 80 percent of victims of Reye's syndrome who go home healthy, she would know what a gift it is to be able to see sunlight and shadow, feel a breeze, smell the damp earth. Perhaps Lee alive would rush by the maple tree, not stop to speculate on the weight of sunlight, but the Lee that lives in memory always seems especially sensitive to beauty in the commonplace, made wise by her death.

When she was only two months dead, I was walking home from the university on Faculty Road when the darkness that had shaded every color since she left began to clear. I had to squint against the unexpected increase of light and felt that Lee was releasing me from mourning and telling me to remember her by celebrating the ordinary. Nothing is obvious, not worthy of attention. Do not take life for granted.

The gift left by a child, partner, parent, brother, sister, colleague, or friend is always a heightened awareness of life. Sometimes we feel guilty about the surge of life energy that follows the death of someone close. We are more aware of life since they can no longer share our renewed delight in the commonplace.

In combat we are usually numbed to the death around us, ignoring the wounded, dying, and the dead, as we pass by. But I suspect each of us who has been under fire has secretly experienced exhilaration at our living while others have died. I once published a poem:

SPRING MORNING 1945

> *I have never*
> *been so alive*
> *as when I woke*
> *among the dying*
> *and the dead.*

Until I wrote that poem it was a secret buried deeply in memory. I didn't feel a surge of renewed life after Lee died, but I did have, beginning on that afternoon walk along Faculty Road, a slowly increasing awareness of the world around me. I would feel the warmth of sunlight on my forearm, the cool of shadow halfway to my elbow, and take account of it. I would catch out of the corner of my eye a moving ocean of farmland, as I had seen in Vermont the day we got the call, stop the car, and study the moving patterns of green, brown, yellow.

Sometimes I would share the texture of tree bark with Lee, pointing out how a fragment of bark appeared to be an island in a surging sea. Other times I just leaned into a winter wind, experiencing life by proxy, enjoying the icy rain that would never pepper Lee's cheeks. I would remember what someone said of her, and I would listen to the Brahms serenades she may not have heard as if I could preserve them for her.

Months or years later—I do not know when—I found I had made another choice: not to mourn but to live more fully than I had before in celebration of Lee's life by taking delight in nature, in music, in people as she had. I like the word *celebration* too much, according to one of my editors, but it means "to respect." I want to respect life, to live more fully, as Lee would want me to. It is not that I can live her life, but I can live my own as best I can in honor of her.

The celebration begins when I wake. I get up at five-thirty, before first light most of the year, and on the mornings I wake with despair, I make myself pay attention. Life is fragile. I study the form of my wife under the covers, often thinking of Rembrandt's sketches of Sasha, his wife, and think how fortunate I have been in this second marriage, now half a century long.

I go downstairs into my shadowed house. Mine. I allow myself a serving of satisfaction. My father, and as far as I know my grandfathers and their fathers, never owned a house. I take possession of this house in the morning. It is the single-family house I dreamed of when I was told to be quiet because of the people who lived upstairs or down. I had come home from the war and gone to college not for scholarship but to earn a place in the middle class, a single-family house with a car in the garage.

I sit on the enclosed porch, windows on three sides, and enjoy the mystery of the light before sunlight, which seems to rise from between the trees in my woods. I go out in that rising light that will suddenly disappear in the explosion of light from the rising sun.

And if there is no sunrise, I take pleasure in the grays of the looming clouds, pay attention to mist and fog, marking the difference, even welcome the many kinds of rain that may fall, and freezing rain and sleet and snow, each bringing its own beauty. I especially enjoy the black lace woven from the silhouettes of winter trees, and some mornings my woods are trimmed with glistening ice.

No one has known—perhaps I have not known until I write this—that the quiet time alone with which I prefer to start my day is a memorial to Lee, not in a mourning sense but a celebration of the life I have been given that was so cruelly taken from her. Perhaps that is why I do not feel lonely when alone.

It is my custom, whenever possible, to share materials on writing with those young and not-so-young who hope to write. And, of course, I complain at the pile of obligation that I have assigned myself when I do not get those materials in the mail right away. Minnie Mae asks why I offer to send things to people when it seems to be such a burden. There are many reasons, but the most important reason, and the one I have not admitted to anyone until now, is that in reaching out I remember Lee. It is what other musicians would have done for her, what she would have done when she became a master of her craft.

Lee often stands just outside the door to my office or comes in quietly and sits in the chair to my left and slightly behind me, sometimes even stands at my shoulder reading what I am writing. It is almost always at a moment of craft when I take delight in an unexpected turn of phrase, a line that suddenly runs clear, a word I have never used in quite that way before.

This sharing is not unique to her. When the writing goes well, I often feel that I am sharing a moment of shaping or the insight that is revealed by the flow of language as I discover what I know that I didn't know. I can go upstairs to find Minnie Mae, pick up the phone or write an e-mail to others. Lee does not answer the phone and doesn't even know what e-mail is, but she is no less there, no farther away as I write.

Say it. Lee's death, the most terrible experience of my life, has also been a gift, a reminder of how important it is that I support and love my wife, daughters, sons-in-law, grandchildren, friends, neighbors, colleagues, and even the passing stranger. She has left us with a continuous celebration of the commonplace.

24. Not Forgetting

It is hard for me to confess how I felt about parents who lost children before we lost Lee. I felt sorry for them, of course, and each time it happened the earth seemed to shift under my feet a bit. I could not imagine how we would survive the loss of Anne, Lee, or Hannah.

When we visited my brother-in-law's house, however, there was a picture on the mantel of Larry, the son they lost to polio during World War II, long before I knew Minnie Mae. I was sure it was a terrible loss, but it seemed that they had erected a shrine to his memory and that his young brothers, one born quite a while after Larry's death, had to compete with this sibling, who could do no wrong. They never seemed to get over Larry's death, although they lived more years after he was gone than they had before. I hope I never felt they should get over it, but I fear I did.

And now I had pictures of Lee in our living room. We hoped that we did not enshrine her memory and make it impossible for Anne and Hannah to compete with their sister, who could no longer make mistakes, fail, be mean or thoughtless or spiteful. I hope we did that, but we did not get over the loss of Lee.

I wondered if we could, and if we should. No one told us to snap out of it, but I feared our grieving would become boring to our friends. Should we close that awful chapter and get on with life? When I mentioned our loss in a column, the mail would come in from others who shared this special grieving, and most of them wondered if they would ever get over it.

In responding to them, I imagined my memories of Lee fading. Her glasses, her face, the way her hair fell toward her shoulders, how she walked. Her smile. The intensity when she practiced the oboe. Her thoughtfulness, her temper, her tears. All gone. Erased. Forgotten.

Not remembered, Lee would not appear in my dreams, never come quietly into my office and sit while I wrote. I would never imagine I saw her walking across campus, noticed her driving by in a car we no longer owned, heard her practicing in the other room.

I would never feel the guilt at not staying by her bed in the hospital, never relive the blurred days after her death when I felt that I was walking in an ocean of molasses, never feel the always unexpected, always painful sense of emptiness at her passing so many years ago.

To those who wrote asking for help in getting over it, I gave this counsel: Imagine that you could forget. Think how terrible it would be not to dream, not to remember, not to miss, not to be sad, not live with this lively shadow that no one else can see by your side, always alive in memory, laughing, teasing, worrying, suffering, sharing the life you go on living.

Remembering may be a celebration or it may be a dagger in the heart, but it is better, far better, than forgetting.

ABOUT THE AUTHOR

Pulitzer Prize–winning journalist Donald M. Murray writes the weekly "Now and Then" column for *The Boston Globe*. *Boston Magazine* and *The Improper Bostonian* magazine selected him best columnist in Boston in 1991 and 1996, respectively. He is professor emeritus of English at the University of New Hampshire, which opened the Donald M. Murray Journalism Laboratory in 1997. His books include *My Twice-Lived Life*, *Write to Learn*, *The Craft of Revision*, *Writing to Deadline*, and *Crafting a Life in Essay, Story, Poem*.